The Whole30 Instant Pot Ultimate Cookbook 2021

365-Days Easy & Delicious Recipes for Quick Detox and Loss Weight

Estelle Artman

TABLE OF CONTENTS

INTRODUCTION

The Whole30 diet is eating genuine nourishment, which means foods with not many fixings or doesn't have a rundown of fixings since they are entire and not handled. Think moderate parts of meat, fish, and eggs; heaps of vegetables; some organic product; a lot of regular fats; and herbs, flavors, and seasonings. Evacuating incendiary foods and drinks in your eating routine ie: sugars, sugars, liquor, grains, vegetables, dairy, heated merchandise and obviously, shoddy nourishment. Regularly you eat three "clean" suppers daily, made with Whole30-endorsed fixings.

Whole30 is a dietary program intended to enable you to eat more beneficial and take out your own trigger nourishments these could be foods that reason a fiery or immune system reaction in your body, or basically foods that reason you to lose all restraint.

For 30 days, you will remove all grains, vegetables, soy, dairy, liquor, included sugars, counterfeit sugars, and handled nourishments containing any of these fixings; and burden upon a wide range of vegetables, natural products, eggs, quality meats and fish, nuts, seeds, and solid fats.

The thought is that, following a month, you'll free yourself of sugar and carb yearnings and begin to truly see the constructive outcomes of receiving an entire nourishments-based eating regimen regardless of whether that is doing better, thinking all the more plainly, feeling less enlarged, or having all the more a punch in your progression.

After the initial 30 days are up, you're urged to gradually reintroduce certain foods each one, in turn, to recognize explicit things that might cause undesirable symptoms and, in this way, what nourishments you most likely need to dump for good.

The Whole30 regularly alluded to as a stricter type of Paleo is a 30-day clean-eating plan that removes nourishments that may unleash devastation on your body. In that manner, the Whole30 is fundamentally the same as the Bulletproof Diet. Individuals utilize the Whole30 as a body reset or even a down-and-messy weight reduction plan.

BENEFITS OF WHOLE30 DIET

More or less, in light of the fact that it thoroughly patches up your association with nourishment, whole30 isn't an eating routine in the conventional sense. You're not permitted to gauge yourself, and excluding calories and estimating bits aren't empowered either.

The genuine objective is to wipe out nourishments that are master incendiary and potential allergens, to recalibrate your taste buds so you normally desire fewer desserts and starches, and to break the passionate ties you may have with certain "comfort" foods that have crashed your dietary patterns previously.

You'll rest longer and all the more soundly: Chicken sugar is out and protein/fat is in, you rest the rest of the equitable.

You'll appreciate predictable vitality: Forget vitality that pinnacles and drops like an exciting ride; you'll become a slug train.

You'll wake up inclination idealistic and alert: There is nothing, and I amount to nothing, superior to awakening with a grin and open heart.

You'll bid a fond farewell to stomach related trouble: Forget about farts and belly thundering and... we should call them "awkward restroom encounters." You may have a little uneasiness at first in case you're not used to eating heaps of veggies, however from that point forward, it's smooth cruising. Your gut will feel greatly improved!

You'll be more joyful: No joke. At the point chicken glucose is steady, life is more joyful. That is all.

You'll be increasingly tranquil: The swirly considerations and uneasiness that can be expedited by the sugar joyride vaporize and leave quiet afterward.

You'll be all the more composed: Goodbye, cerebrum mist, and tip-of-the-tongue disorder! Hi

You'll drink more water: Sugary beverages are out, so you'll normally end up drinking more water which is a splendid thing for making your body work at the ideal limit.

You'll eat more vegetables: Get prepared to eat like a rabbit! You'll be eating around a few measures of veggies for each feast. Per. Supper. Think about every one of the supplements.

You'll enjoy your food more: For me, sparkling the focus on quality nourishment causes me to value its nutritive power and flavor more than expected. I back off, appreciate each nibble, and consider how it's created me solid while it tastes so damn great.

You'll feel the contrast between passionate craving and genuine appetite: You realize that thoughtless eating that happens chicken you're focused or occupied? That is enthusiastic hunger, and it's junky. During the Whole30, as your body gets off the sugar rush and subsides into better insulin the board, your craving begins to decrease, however genuine yearning the requirement for quality nourishment that sign chicken it's an ideal opportunity to eat kicks in. It feels so great.

You'll discover new most loved foods: Who knows which vegetables, flavors, and meat arrangements will turn into your top choices?! It's energizing to consider, no? There's such a great amount of room in your chicken and on your plate for new taste sensations chicken you exile the grains, beans, and dairy.

You'll have a ton of fun testing in the chicken: The Whole30 is basically what got me into the chicken and playing with plans. I was enlivened to perceive what I could do with vegetable +meat +fat, and I urge you to do likewise. Give the Whole30 and Well Fed 2 a chance to enable you to play with your food.

You'll turn out to be increasingly sorted out: somewhat, the Whole30 expects you to grasp intending to guarantee your prosperity, and that dimension of association can stream into different aspects of your life, as well.

You'll know genuine resolution: Most of us will in general reprimand ourselves for "absence of determination," however actually a lot of our thoughtless eating is driven by our hormones. Chicken we deal with our hormonal reaction by eating the correct nourishment, the right messages about yearning are conveyed through our bodies. No superhuman, poise required!

You'll find out about yourself: By concentrating on your propensities for 30 days, you'll gain proficiency with a wide range of things, including what triggers your hunger, who's a piece of your emotionally supportive network, what you require for self-consideration, what time of day you go to the washroom, and that's just the beginning!

You'll kill the sugar evil presence: Vanquish that trouble maker! And afterward, later, on the off chance that you go head to head with the Sugar Demon once more, you'll realize that it's inside your capacity to take a sword to his carotid chicken the opportunity arrives.

You'll make new companions: There's an enormous network of Whole30 members on the web and disconnected, and during your Whole30, you can take advantage of their help, information, comical inclination, triumphs, and difficulties.

You'll decidedly impact others: Yes, you'll unavoidably get the "You have to eat entire grains." contention from some good-natured colleagues, and that will irritate. Be that as it may, on the off chance that you discreetly adhere to your program, you'll likewise positively affect the general population around you chicken they see your outcomes. I can't reveal to you what number of individuals was desirous of my Whole30 pressed snacks in my office, and that is a non-confrontational approach to open the way to an extraordinary discussion.

You'll become familiar with how your body functions: This is a two-overlay win. To begin with, by understanding the standards of the science behind the Whole30, you'll become familiar with somewhat about how human bodies capacity, and second, you'll figure out how you an extraordinary, exceptional snowflake work specifically.

WHAT YOU CAN EAT ON WHOLE30

After that truly debilitating rundown of foods, you can't eat; it may appear a touch of overwhelming to begin the program. Be that as it may, there are as yet a lot of tasty fixings that can contain an incredible dinner.

Vegetables: Eat vegetables including potatoes! However much you might want.

Fruits: Fruits are permitted, with some restraint. Keep in mind that you're attempting to restrain your sugar admission during the 30 days.

Unprocessed Meats: Sausage is still alright, yet check for included sugar and other off-limit additives.

Seafood: Fish and shellfish get the Whole30 thumbs up.

Eggs: Eggs will turn into your new breakfast beastie.

Nuts and seeds: All nuts and seeds are alright, with one special case: peanuts, since they are a vegetable.

Oils and ghee: Just express yes to olive oil and coconut oil. Ghee, which is a sort of explained spread, is likewise permitted.

Coffee: Yes, you can have an espresso while on Whole30, however, you can't include any milk items or sugar to help it up. Take a stab at making your own almond milk.

FOODS TO KEEP AWAY FROM ON WHOLE30

Added sugar, genuine or fake: This incorporates (yet isn't restricted to) maple syrup, nectar, agave nectar, coconut sugar, date syrup, Stevie, priest organic product, Splendid, Equal.

Alcohol: Any type of liquor is a no go, notwithstanding for cooking.

Grains: All grains are forbidden (even without gluten grains!), including wheat, rye, grain, oats, corn, rice, millet, bulgur, sorghum, grew grains, quinoa, and buckwheat.

Legumes: This incorporates beans of different types, peas, chickpeas, lentils, peanuts, and nutty spread.

Dairy. Milk, cream, cheddar, kefir, yogurt, acrid cream, dessert, or solidified yogurt.

Certain added substances: Carrageen an, MSG, and sulfites are every one of the no go.

Baked merchandise, low-quality nourishments, or even treats with "affirmed" fixings

INSTANT POT BREAKFAST RECIPES

Instant pot Scotch Eggs

Prep Time: 15mins, Cooking Time: 10mins, Serving: 4

INGREDIENTS

- 4 - large eggs
- 1 - lb. country style ground sausage
- 1 - Tablespoon vegetable oil

INSTRUCTIONS

1. Put a steamer basket within the weight cooker pot. Include 1 glass water and the eggs. Lock top set up, cook dinner on High Pressure for 6mins.
2. At the factor whilst clock signals, permit the burden discharge normally for 6mins. At that point mood killer weight cooker and whole a snappy weight discharge.
3. At the point while the weight is discharged, cautiously expel the pinnacle. Expel the steamer container from the weight cooking pot.
4. Place eggs into excellent bloodless water to chill.
5. At the factor chicken the eggs are cool evacuate the shells. Partition the frankfurter into 4 equal pieces. Level each piece right into a level round.
6. Spot the difficult bubbled egg within the middle and delicately fold the hotdog over the egg.
7. Warmth the burden cooking pot on sauté or searing. At the point while the pot is warm, include oil and dark colored the Scotch eggs on 4 sides.
8. Put a rack in the weight cooking pot and see the Scotch Eggs on the rack.
9. Lock the pinnacle installation and weight prepare dinner on high weight for 6 minutes.
10. At the factor chicken clock signals, entire a fast weight discharge. At the point whilst the load is discharged, carefully evacuate the quilt.

Nutrition Fact: Calories 414.3g, Fat 17.3g, Carbs 35.2g, Sugars 1.8g, Protein 39.8g

Instant Pot Greek Yogurt

Prep Time: 5mins, Cooking Time: 35mins, Servings: 14

INGREDIENTS

- 1 - Gallon Whole Milk
- 2 - Tablespoons Yogurt "Starter"

INSTRUCTIONS

1. Add some water to the Instant Pot cooking pot, lock on the cover and close Pressure Valve. Push the Steam catch and modify time to 5 minutes. At the point chicken Beep is heard, open Pressure Valve.

2. Empty Milk into cold/cool Pressure Cooker cooking pot. Spread with IP Lid or Glass Lid. Close the Pressure Valve, chicken ever wanted.

3. Push Yogurt catch and afterward the Adjust catch, until it says "boil."Multiple times during bubble cycle, expel cover and whisk Milk.

4. At the point chicken Beep sounds, open cover, whisk and take the temperature. In the event that the temperature isn't 180 degrees, rehash the last advance or utilize the Sauté/Low capacity to get it up to temp, whisking persistently.

5. At the point chicken 180 degrees is achieved, expel cooking pot and spot in chicken sink loaded with virus water. Chill Milk off to 95-110 degrees, whisking frequently.

6. Temper starter - scoop out some Milk and rush in the Starter. Empty Milk once again into the cooking pot, whisk all together.

7. Spot cooking pot again into the Instant Pot and spread with IP Lid or Glass Lid. Press Yogurt catch.

8. The presentation screen will say 8:00. Ensure show says "Ordinary." Use the +/ - catch to alter time to your ideal dimension of pungency.

9. At the point chicken Cycle closes, evacuate cooking pot to fridge, until cool, 6-8 hours.

10. Utilize a Yogurt Strainer and strain the yogurt in the cooler for in any event two hours. Your whey ought to be translucent/clear. In the event that the whey is overcast, include another layer of cheesecloth/spread muslin to your stressing gadget. The Euro Strainer should deliver clear whey.

Nutrition Facts: Calories 166g, Fat 8g, Carbs 13g, Sugars 9g, Protein 8g

Ham, Egg, and Cheese Casserole

Prep Time: 15mins, Cooking Time: 15mins, Serving: 5-6

INGREDIENTS

- 32 - ounce bag frozen cubed hash browns
- 1 - large onion diced
- 1-2 - cups Cooked and Crumbled Turkey Breakfast Sausage
- 2 - cups shredded cheddar cheese
- 10-12 large eggs
- 1 - cup whole milk
- 1 - teaspoon salt
- 1 - teaspoon pepper

INSTRUCTIONS

1. Shower the addition of a slight cooker, moment pot, or five-quart dutch stove with nonstick cooking splash. Spot 1/3 of hash tans within the base. Top with 1/three onions, 1/3 ham, and 1/3 cheddar. Rehash two additional activities.

2. In an great blending bowl, beat collectively eggs, milk, salt, and pepper until all round blended. Pour over ham and potato layers.

3. To make in a broiler: Bake, found out, at 325 for an hour and a 1/2, or until the eggs are set.

4. To make in a slight cooker: Place field in a moderate cooker, spread with cowl, and heat on low 7-eight hours or excessive, 3-4 hours.

5. To make in an Instant Pot: Place embed in Instant Pot. Press "Moderate Cooker", at that factor "Alter" till the light is going beforehand underneath "much less", alter time using further to and short signal to get it to 7 hours. In the event which you'd like to cook it faster, press "Moderate Cooker", do not acclimate to less, at that factor regulate time to 3-4 hours.

Nutrition Fact: Calories 318.5g, Fat 12.5g, Carbs 29.6g, Sugars 1.8g, Protein 20.2g

Korean Style Steamed Eggs

Prep Time: 5mins, Cooking Time: 5mins, Serving: 4

INGREDIENTS

- 1 - Large egg
- 1/3 - Cup cold water
- 1 - tsp Chopped scallions
- Pinch of sesame seeds
- Pinch of garlic powder salt and pepper

INSTRUCTIONS

1. Blend the egg and water in a little bowl
2. Strain the egg blend over a fine work strainer into a heatproof bowl
3. Include the remainder of the fixings and blend well and put aside.
4. Add 1 Cup of water to the inward pot of Instant Pot
5. Spot the trivet or a steamer bin in the pot
6. Spot the bowl with the egg blend on the trivet or a steamer bin.
7. Close the top firmly, close the vent valve.
8. Press "Manual" setting on HIGH and set the clock for 5 minutes.
9. At the point chicken the clock goes off, discharge the weight physically
10. Serve quickly with hot rice

Nutrition Fact: Calories 212.7g, Fat 10.1g, Carbs 14.3g, Sugars 1.9g, Protein 15.8g

Instant pot Breakfast Quinoa

Prep Time: 5mins, Cooking Time: 10mins, Serving: 3-5

INGREDIENTS

- 1 ½ - cups uncooked quinoa
- 2 ¼ - cups water
- 2 - Tablespoons maple syrup

- ½ - teaspoon vanilla
- ¼ - teaspoon ground cinnamon
- Pinch of salt
- Toppings: milk, fresh berries

INSTRUCTIONS

1. Include quinoa, water, maple syrup, vanilla, cinnamon, and salt to the weight cooking pot.
2. Select high weight and 1 moment Cooking Time. At the point chicken signal sounds turn weight cooker off, hold up 10 minutes, and after that utilization a Quick Pressure Release to discharge any outstanding weight.
3. At the point chicken valve drops cautiously evacuate cover, tilting far from you to enable steam to scatter.
4. Lighten the quinoa and serve hot with milk, berries, and cut almonds.

Nutrition Fact: Calories 247.1g, Fat 17.3g, Carbs 1.2g, Sugars 0.3g, Protein 21.1g

Instant Pot Steel Cut Oats

Prep Time: 5mins, Cooking Time: 3mins, Serving: 4

INGREDIENTS

- 1 - Cup steel cut oats
- 3 - Cups water

INSTRUCTIONS

1. Pour steel reduce oats within the metallic pot.
2. Include 3 bins of water.
3. Secure the cover, press guide, and set time to 3mins.
4. Enable the Instant Pot to come back to weight - kind of 5mins.
5. Chicken ever finished function discharge weight - round 5-10mins.
6. Include fixings on every occasion desired, and admire

Nutrition Fact: Calories 375.7g, Fat 17.2g, Carbs 32g, Sugars 3.7g, Protein 24.2g

Easy Instant Pot Applesauce

Prep Time: 10mins, Cooking Time: 10mins, Servings: 8

INGREDIENTS

- 3 - lb apples cored
- 1 - tbsp apple pie spice
- 1 - tbsp ghee
- pinch cloves & pinch sea salt
- 2 - star anise optional & ½ - cup water

INSTRUCTIONS

1. Include the slashed apples, crusty fruit-filled treat zest, ghee, cloves, ocean salt and celebrity anise to the Instant Pot.
2. Toss the entirety to consolidate, at that factor consist of half of glass water.
3. Manual is excessive weight.
4. After the cycle completes, allow the strain to discharge normally for at any rate 15mins.
5. Squash the apples as finely as you want, and whilst the fruit purée is cool sufficient, contain it.

Nutrition Facts: Calories 108g, Fat 2g, Carbs 24g, Sugars 17g, Protein 32g

Instant Pot Crispy Potatoes

Prep Time: 20mins, Cooking Time: 15mins, Serving: 4

INGREDIENTS

- 1 - pound fingerling or Yukon Gold potatoes
- 2 - tablespoons of ghee, avocado oil
- Kosher salt
- Freshly ground black pepper
- ¼ cup minced chives or Italian parsley
- Juice from ½ medium lemon

INSTRUCTIONS

1. Add some water to the cooking supplement of an Instant Pot.
2. Cooker fitted with a steamer embed.

Nutrition Fact: Calories 423g, Fat 35.3g, Carbs 5.2g, Sugars 1.2g, Protein 21.3g

Instant Pot Paleo Breakfast Casserole

Prep Time: 15mins, Cooking Time: 25mins, Serving: 6

INGREDIENTS

- 2 - tablespoons Coconut Oil
- 1 ⅓ - cups slice Leek
- 2 - teaspoons mince Garlic
- 1 - cup chop Kale
- 8 - individual Egg
- ⅔ - cups peel and grate Sweet Potato
- 1 ½ - cups cook Sausage

INSTRUCTIONS

1. Set Instant Pot to sauté and dissolve coconut oil in an inward pot.

2. Include leeks, garlic, and kale and sauté until diminished.
3. Expel sautéed vegetables from inward pot and clean.
4. In an enormous bowl, join eggs, sweet potato, wiener, and sautéed vegetables.
5. Empty blend into a lubed broiler verification container/bowl.
6. Add water and trivet to the inward pot. Make a foil sling to bring down the container onto the trivet. Lock top into spot and seal steam spout.
7. Set on high weight for 25 minutes.
8. Snappy discharge weight.
9. Cut into equivalent cuts.

Nutrition Facts: Calories 280g, Fat 19g, Carbs 7g, Sugar 2g, Protein 25g

Instant Pot Egg Bites

Prep Time: 25mins, Cooking Time: 10mins, Serving: 8

INGREDIENTS

- 8 - large eggs
- ¼ - cup milk
- ¼ - teaspoon salt
- 1/8 - teaspoon freshly ground black pepper
- ½ - cup diced ham or precooked bacon
- 1/3 - cup shredded cheddar cheese
- 1 - green onion

INSTRUCTIONS

1. Liberally splash silicone infant sustenance plate with nonstick cooking bathe.
2. In a massive bowl, whisk the eggs, milk, salt, and pepper until sincerely mixed. Uniformly partition the beef among silicone glasses.
3. Sprinkle the cheddar over every egg nibble.
4. Empty 1 container water into the burden cooking pot and see a trivet inside the base.
5. Utilize a sling to carry down the silicone plate, cautiously stacking one over the alternative. Lock the duvet installation.
6. Select High Pressure and eleven minutes cook dinner time for firmer egg chomps.
7. At the factor chicken the cooking time closes, flip off the weight cooker.
8. Give the weight a hazard to discharge typically for 5mins, at that point entire with a fast weight discharge.
9. At the point chicken the valve drops, carefully expel the duvet and utilize the sling to evacuate the plate.
10. Spot on a wire rack to cool for 5mins, at that point flip the plate over and delicately crush to expel the egg chomps from the silicone plate.

11. Serve egg chomps whole or cut over scaled down croissants or toast.

Nutrition Fact: Calories 218g, Fat 15g, Carbs 19g, Sugars 1.2g, Protein 22g

Egg Muffins in the instant pot

Prep Time: 20mins, Cooking Time: 30mins, Serving: 4

INGREDIENTS

- 4 - eggs
- ¼ - teaspoon lemon pepper seasoning
- 4 - tablespoons shredded cheddar/Jack cheese
- 1 - green onion, 4 - slices precooked bacon

INSTRUCTIONS

1. Put the steamer crate inside the weight cooker pot and consist of half of glasses water.
2. Break eggs into a huge estimating bowl with pour gush, consist of lemon pepper, and beat well.
3. Partition the cheddar, bacon and green onion equally between the four silicone biscuit mugs.
4. Empty the overwhelmed eggs into each biscuit glass and blend with a fork to consolidate.
5. Spot biscuit mugs on steamer container. Spread and lock pinnacle installation. Select High Pressure and 8mins Cooking Time.
6. At the factor whilst clock signals, flip off, maintain up minutes, and at that factor make use of a handy guide a rough weight discharge.
7. Cautiously open the cover, carry out the steamer bin, and evacuate biscuit packing containers.
8. Serve promptly or biscuits will hold over seven days in the icebox.
9. Microwave on excessive round 30 seconds to heat.

Nutrition Facts: Calories 410g, Fat 13g, Carbs 61g, Sugar 18g, Protein 12g

Instant Pot Coconut Yogurt

Prep Time: 2hrs 40mins, Cooking Time: 5hrs 50mins, Serving: 3-4

INGREDIENTS

- 1 - L coconut cream
- 1 - package yogurt starter with live cultures
- 1 - tbsp grass-fed gelatin
- 3 - half pint jars and lids

INSTRUCTIONS

1. This wills warmness it to the factor of boiling.

2. At the point whilst the readout changes to "Yogurt", expel the liner from the pot, turn off the Instant Pot.

3. Give the now fluid coconut a hazard to cream cool, either at the counter or ice chest so the temperature drops to underneath 100F.

4. This is a vast increase, excessively warm, and your yogurt won't a way of life and be tart, you need the right temperature so you do not murder the live societies.

5. Chicken the coconut milk is the best temperature, rush inside the starter a bit at any given moment, no protuberances.

6. Press the "Yogurt" trap and regulate the time, the extra you place the clock, the tangier it'll be.

7. Eight hours is precisely how I love it, I turn it on earlier than mattress, it's prepared before sunrise!

8. While it's far nevertheless heated, race inside the gelatin a little at any given second, again you do not need clusters.

9. Empty in addition into the bins leaving area for the correct fixings.

10. Put on the quilt and refrigerate 4-6 hours, it's going to set up to a thick tart Greek-fashion coconut yogurt.

11. Blend a long time earlier than serving.

Nutrition Fact: Calories 425.2g, Fat 6g, Carbs 12g, Sugars 2.4g, Protein 28g

Instant Pot Vegan Pumpkin Coffeecake Steel-cut Oatmeal

Prep Time: 5mins, Cooking Time: 5mins, Servings: 6

INGREDIENTS

- 4 ½ - cups water
- 1 ½ - cups steel-cut oats
- 1 ½ - cups pumpkin puree
- 2 - teaspoons cinnamon
- 1 - teaspoon allspice
- 1 - teaspoon vanilla

Coffee Cake Topping:

- ½ - cup coconut sugar
- ¼ - cup pecans
- 1 - tablespoon cinnamon

INSTRUCTIONS

1. Include all the moment pot fixings to your treated steel supplement and place it into the base. Secure the cover and ensure the valve is shut. Set on manual and cook for 3 minutes.

2. While the oats are cooking, combine all the fixing fixings and store in an impermeable compartment.

3. Chicken the oats are cooked, enable the strain to descend normally. Chicken the silver weight pointer goes down you can open the cover.

4. Serve sprinkled with garnish and additionally your most loved nondairy milk

Nutrition Fact: Calories 254g, Fat 5g, Carbs 45g, Sugar 11g, Protein 7g

Easy Instant Pot Blueberry Jam

Prep Time: 25mins, Cooking Time: 20mins, Serving: 3

INGREDIENTS

- 2 - pounds blueberries fresh
- 1 - pound raw honey local

INSTRUCTIONS

1. Add blueberries to an inward pot of Instant Pot.
2. Put weight cooker on low warm temperature till nectar softens. In the case of utilizing solidified berries, this part may also take the time, but do not strain.
3. Chickenever dissolved, flip weight cooker to high warm temperature till nectar bubbles.
4. Chicken it bubbles, rapidly put on the pinnacle of your cooker, watching that the seals and all components are fit as a mess around, incorporating being inside the fixing position.
5. On the off risk that utilizing an electric powered cooker, hit the Cancel trap, at that factor set to excessive for 2mins.
6. On the off threat that utilizing a stovetop cooker, deliver to excessive weight and maintain up weight for a Cooking Time of two minutes.
7. Chicken cooking time is completed, if using an electric powered cooker, hit the Cancel trap to mood killer the warm temperature, and unplug.
8. With a stovetop cooker, expel from warm temperature. Let depressurize generally.
9. Chickenever depressurized, expel pinnacle and betray to excessive warm temperature.
10. Let bubble until a part of the water has dissipated off, and the jam is respectable and gelled chicken trickled off a spoon.
11. Make a point to scratch the bottom regularly to assure however gelling.
12. Empty jam into clean half-16 oz. Boxes. Store in the icebox.

Nutrition Fact: Calories 247.1g, Fat 17.3g, Carbs 1.2g, Sugars 0.3g, Protein 21.1g

Apple-Delicata Squash Porridge

Prep Time: 15mins, Cooking Time: 10mins, Servings: 3

INGREDIENTS

- 4 - small or 2 large apples unpeeled
- 1 - delicata squash washed and whole
- ½ - cup bone broth with little fat

- 3 - Tablespoons slippery
- 2 - Tablespoons gelatin
- 2 - Tablespoons maple syrup
- ½ - teaspoon cinnamon
- 1/8 - teaspoon each: cloves and ginger
- pinch sea salt

INSTRUCTIONS

1. Spot entire, whole delicate squash into supplement pot. Include apple lumps. Include bone stock and flavors. Ensure the elastic ring is set up in the Instant Pot cover, and a secure top, shutting steam valve. Pick Manual setting and 8 minutes.

2. At the point chicken the clock goes off, enable the strain to discharge normally for 10 minutes; at that point press Cancel, place a chicken towel over the steam valve and open it to discharge any residual weight. Evacuate cover and supplement, so the pot's substance starts to cool.

3. At the point chicken cool enough to deal with, place delicate on a plate or cutting board. Cut down the middle length-wise and expel seeds with a spoon. Spot squash parts and pot's substance into a blender.

4. Include remaining fixings: discretionary tricky elm, gelatin, maple syrup, and ocean salt. Mix for around 30 seconds, until smooth. Present with discretionary fixings, or fill versatile holders for pressing in snacks.

Nutrition Fact: Calories 247.1g, Fat 17.3g, Carbs 1.2g, Sugars 0.3g, Protein 21.1g

instat pot Crustless Meat Lovers Quiche

Prep Time: 15mins, Cooking Time: 30mins, Serving: 5

INGREDIENTS

- 6 - large eggs, well beaten
- ½ - cup milk
- ¼ - teaspoon salt
- 1/8 - teaspoon ground black pepper
- 4 - slices bacon
- 1 - cup cooked ground sausage
- ½ - cup diced ham
- 2 - large green onions
- 1 - cup shredded cheese

INSTRUCTIONS

1. Put a steel trivet within the base of the load cooking pot and encompass 1 container water.

2. In a 1-quart soufflé dish, include bacon, wiener, ham, green onions, and cheddar and blend nicely.

3. Pour egg blend over to the pinnacle of the beef and blend to consolidate.

4. Freely unfold the soufflé dish with aluminum foil.

5. Focus the soufflé dish on a foil sling and carefully decrease it onto the trivet in the cooking pot.

6. Select High Pressure and 30 minutes prepare dinner time.

7. At the point whilst the cooking time closes, permit the stress to discharge generally for 10mins, at that point entire with a fast weight discharge.

8. At the point chicken the valve drops, cautiously open the top. Lift out the soufflé dish and expel the foil.

9. Chicken ever wanted, sprinkle the very best factor of the quiche with extra cheddar and cook dinner until dissolved and daintily sautéed.

10. Serve right away.

Nutrition Fact: Calories 423g, Fat 33g, Carbs 15g, Sugars 3.1g, Protein 36g

Instant pot Spanish Tortilla Potato Egg Frittata

Prep Time: 10mins, Cooking Time: 18mins, Servings: 4

INGREDIENTS

- 6 - large Eggs
- 4 - oz French Fries
- 1 - Tablespoon Butter melted
- ¼ - cup Spanish Onions Scallions
- ½ - teaspoon Sea Salt
- ¼ - teaspoon Freshly Ground Black Pepper
- 1 - teaspoon Fox Point Seasoning
- 1 - clove Fresh Garlic
- ¼ - cup Milk
- 1 - teaspoon Tomato Paste
- 4 - oz Cheese grated
- 1.5 - cups Water

Topping:

- 1 - oz Cheese If desired

INSTRUCTIONS

1. Strip and cut potatoes into dainty strips and absorb water for 20 minutes.

2. In a medium bowl, whisk together eggs and seasonings until foamy.

3. In a blending container, whisk together, tomato glue and milk and add to egg blend. Whisk well. Add onions and garlic to egg blend.

4. Altogether oil goulash dish. Expel potatoes from water and dry with a paper towel. Include crude potatoes and pour in.

5. Pour in egg blend and any include ins and top with cheddar.

6. Add water to Pressure Cooker cooking pot and spot a Trivet. Spot revealed meal dish on Trivet.

7. Lock on top and close Pressure Valve. Cook on High Pressure for 15-20 minutes.

8. At the point chicken Beep sounds, permit a 10-minute Natural Pressure Release and after that discharge the remainder of the weight.

9. Top with ground cheddar (if utilizing) and place Lid over Pressure Cooker and enable cheddar to dissolve.

Nutrition Fact: Calories 212.7g, Fat 10.1g, Carbs 14.3g, Sugars 1.9g, Protein 15.8g

Instant Pot Blood Orange Marmalade

Prep Time: 25mins, Cooking Time: 35mins, Serving: 4

INGREDIENTS

- 4 - whole blood oranges
- 1 - lemon, juice of
- 1.5 - weight of fruit in caster sugar

INSTRUCTIONS

1. Begin by gauging the blood oranges and note down the weight. Wash them under hot wash well, scouring to get any wax covering off. Additionally, disinfect your containers.

2. Cut the blood oranges in quarters and cut they as meagerly as you can oversee - utilize a mandolin on the off chance that you are cautious. Dispose of pips.

3. Scoop the cut natural product into the Inner Pot with all their juice in addition to that of the lemon. Include 250ml water and close the cover, setting to 12 minutes Manual (High). Permit an NPR. Drop the Keep Warm capacity

4. Weigh out 1.5 x the heaviness of the oranges in caster sugar and add to the cooked organic product, blending to enable it to break down.

5. Press Sauté and blending always to abstain from getting and consuming on the base of the pot, heat until moment read thermometer indicates 104.5°C. Remove the warmth and permit cooling quickly while you recover your sterile containers from the broiler/dishwasher If wishing to make shred less jelly, essentially go it through a fine fit sifter, squeezing immovably to guarantee as much mash experiences simply deserting the strip. Scratch the jam off the underside of the sifter. Spoon into the hot sterile containers, fixing the tops right away. In the event that leaving the strip in, at that point basically scoop into containers, endeavoring to disseminate the strip equally between them.

Nutrition Fact: Calories 318.5g, Fat 12.5g, Carbs 29.6g, Sugars 1.8g, Protein 20.2g

Instant pot Spiced Pumpkin Apple Butter

Prep Time: 20mins, Cooking Time: 15mins, Serving: 4-5

INGREDIENTS

- 2 – cans pumpkin puree
- 1 - Tablespoon pumpkin pie spice
- 3 - Peeled and cored apples
- 1 - Cup white sugar
- ½ - cup honey
- 1 – 12 -oz bottle hard apple cider
- Pinch of salt

INSTRUCTIONS

1. Join all fixings in weight cooker, blend, and set to high weight for 10 minutes.
2. At the point chicken time is up, complete a characteristic discharge for 15 minutes and after that a snappy discharge for any residual weight.
3. Scoop margarine into artisan containers or other sealed shut compartments and let cool totally before refrigerating.
4. Refrigerate until prepared to serve.
5. Eat inside 2-3 weeks

Nutrition Fact: Calories 345g, Fat 7g, Carbs 12g, Sugars 0.1g, Protein 21g

Instant Pot Blueberry Breakfast

Prep Time: 6mins, Cooking Time: 6mins, Serving: 6

INGREDIENTS

- 1/3 - cup old fashioned oats
- 1/3 - cup unsweetened almond milk
- 1/3 - cup fat free Greek yogurt
- 1/3 - cup blueberries
- 1 - Tablespoon chia seeds
- Sweetener to taste
- Splash of vanilla
- Pinch of mineral salt
- Sprinkle of cinnamon
- 1-1/2 cups of water for the pot

INSTRUCTIONS

1. Pour water in your vacant pot and put aside.
2. Utilizing a somewhat little container, pour in all fixings in the request given.

3. Spread top of the container with a bit of aluminum foil and spot in the pot.
4. Set physically for 6 minutes.
5. Enable your moment pot to discharge weight normally.
6. Utilizing a pot holder or stove glove, cautiously take out container and set it on the counter to cool for a couple of minutes.
7. Chicken cool enough to contact, mix cereal and appreciate

Nutrition Fact: Calories 377g, Fat 12g, Carbs 22g, Sugars 3g, Protein 32g

INSTANT POT DEEF LAMB AND PORK RECIPES

Instant Pot Pork Carnitas Lettuce Wraps Recipe

Prep Time: 20mins, Cooking Time: 40mins, Serves: 6

INGREDIENTS

- 3-4 - lb pork shoulder
- 2 - Tbsp olive oil
- ½ - tsp chili powder
- ½ - tsp smoked paprika
- 1 - tsp cumin
- 1 - tsp salt
- 2 - limes, juiced
- ½ - cup fresh orange juice
- ½ - cup chicken stock
- 1 - tsp parsley
- 1 - tsp minced garlic
- ½ - cup diced onion
- 1 - 2 - T jalapeños
- cilantro and salsa to garnis

INSTRUCTIONS

1. Cut pork in 1" solid shapes and season with salt, cumin, paprika, and bean stew powder.
2. Turn Instant Pot to "sauté ". Chicken hot include oil, juice of 1 lime, and meat. Cook for 5-8 min, sautéing on the two sides.
3. Include remaining lime and squeezed an orange, quartered oranges, chicken stock, garlic, onion, parsley, and jalapeño to meat.
4. Lock top, close weight valve, press "manual" setting, and cook for 30 minutes.
5. Enable strain to discharge normally for 15 minutes, and after that physically discharge remaining.
6. Expel pork from pot and spot on cutting board.
7. Shred pork with a fork
8. Serve inside romaine lettuce leaves, bested with cilantro and salsa. Mango salsa is my top pick, yet any salsa will do.

Nutrition Fact: Calories 473.4g, Fat 25.1g, Carbs 9.2g, Sugars 0.7g, Protein 50.9g

Jamaican Jerk Pork Roast

Prep Time: 15mins, Cooking Time: 45mins, Serving: 12

INGREDIENTS

- 4 - lb pork shoulder
- ¼ - cup Jamaican Jerk spice blend
- 1 - Tbsp olive oil
- ½ - cup beef stock

INSTRUCTIONS

1. Rub the dish with olive oil and coat with Jamaican Jerk flavor mix.
2. Set your Instant Pot to Sauté and dark colored the meat on all sides.
3. Include the meat soup.
4. Seal the top as indicated by directions and cook on Manual, high weight, for 45 minutes.
5. Discharge weight as indicated by directions, shred and serve.

Nutrition Fact: Calories 247.1g, Fat 17.3g, Carbs 1.2g, Sugars 0.3g, Protein 21.1g

90-minute Kalua Pork

Prep Time: 5mins, Cooking Time: 1hr 40mins, Serving: 8

INGREDIENTS

- 4 – 5 - pound pork shoulder
- 1 - teaspoon salt
- ½ - cup diced pineapple
- 1 - Teaspoon fish sauce
- 1 - tablespoon liquid smoke
- ½ - cup water

INSTRUCTIONS

1. Season the red meat with salt and add to the complement of your Instant pot alongside the pineapple, fish sauce, fluid smoke, and water.
2. Lock on the duvet and turn the valve to solving.
3. Cook at a excessive weight for an hour and a half of.
4. Following an hour and a 1/2, permit the steam to discharge generally for 10-15mins, at that factor turn the valve to venting.
5. Expel the red meat from the Instant pot and carefully empty out the juices right into a field.
6. Draw the meat separated with forks, evacuating any abundance fats.
7. Chicken the fats ascents to the best factor of the field, evacuate it with a bit scoop and cast off.

8. Include a portion of the juices returned to the red meat, as desired.

Nutrition Fact: Calories 269.5g, Fat 20.4g, Carbs 6g, Sugars 0.3g, Protein 19.9g

5-Spice Pork Stew Instant Pot

Prep Time: 20mins, Cooking Time: 35mins, Servings: 5

INGREDIENTS

- 2 - lbs boneless organic pork butt
- 2 - tbsp olive oil
- Pinch of sea salt
- 6-8 - boiled chicken eggs
- chopped cilantro leaves and stems

Aromatic base:

- 1 - tbsp dry coriander seeds
- 1 - tbsp ginger
- 1 - tbsp black peppercorns
- 2 - tbsp garlic cloves

Pork stew combo:

- 2 - tbsp 5 spice powder
- 1 ½ - cup coconut aminos
- 4 - tbsp Chinese rice wine
- 2 - tbsp cacao powder
- 2 - tbsp organic raw honey
- 1 ½ - tbsp ginger
- 1 - cup chopped cilantro
- 1 - medium yellow onion
- 1 - in whole garlic head, peeled and sliced half
- 8 - cups tap water
- 1 - tbsp coarse sea salt

INSTRUCTIONS

1. Spot fixings under "sweet-smelling base" in a mortar and pestle.
2. Select a temperature with the "Modify" key for "Typical".
3. At the factor while Instant Pot achieves the given working temperature, it shows "Hot" encompass 2 tbsp of olive oil and you may begin sautéing/cooking meat.
4. We are looking for a mild first-rate darker shading so it should take you around 5 mins aggregate to burn the beef.
5. Season a touch of salt on every facet of pork.

6. Keep the "Sauté" paintings on for the subsequent level.

7. In the event that the pot is dry, include another tbsp of olive oil and sauté the "sweet-smelling base" from degree 1 until fragrant, round three minutes.

8. Add the beef returned to the pot. Include all fixings beneath "Pork stew combination".

9. Cautiously Seal/Lock the weight cooker. Select "Meat/Stew" work key. 35 minutes.

10. Meanwhile, bubble 6-eight chicken eggs on a stovetop. Chickenever cool, strip and positioned aside.

11. At the point whilst the beef is performed, spoon off the top layer of fat superficially.

12. Include the eggs and allow them to soak up juices.

13. Scoop a couple of spoonsful of stew fluid over steamed rice and stewed pork.

14. Sprinkle some cilantro and gift with cured cabbage/cucumber/or undeniable sauerkraut.

Nutrition Fact: Calories 423g, Fat 35.3g, Carbs 5.2g, Sugars 1.2g, Protein 21.3g

Pork Sirloin Roast in the instant pot

Prep Time: 15mins, Cooking Time: 25mins, Serving: 10

INGREDIENTS

- ½ - teaspoon coarse black pepper
- ½ - teaspoon salt
- ½ - teaspoon onion powder
- ½ - teaspoon garlic powder
- ¼ - teaspoon chili powder
- 3 - pound pork sirloin tip roast
- 1 - tablespoon vegetable oil
- 1 - cup water
- ½ - cup apple juice

INSTRUCTIONS

1. Combine flavors in a little bowl and rub zest blend all over pork cook.

2. Place oil in the cooking pot and select sautéing. At the point chicken oil starts to sizzle, dark colored dish on the two sides.

3. Include the water and squeezed apple to the weight cooking pot.

4. Lock cover set up. Select High Pressure and set a 25 moment Cooking Time. At the point chicken the clock sounds, turn off weight cooker and enable the strain to discharge normally for 5 minutes, at that point complete with a brisk weight discharge. At the point chicken valve drops cautiously evacuate the cover.

5. Check the pork with a moment read thermometer- - it ought to be above 145°F. Expel the pork from the weight cooking pot and permit to rest for 3 minutes. Cut meagerly and serve.

Nutrition Fact: Calories 423g, Fat 35.3g, Carbs 5.2g, Sugars 1.2g, Protein 21.3g

Instant Pot Pulled Pork

Prep Time: 20mins, Cooking Time: 1hr 10mins, Servings: 10

INGREDIENTS

For the Pork:

- 4 - lb. boneless pork shoulder
- Pork rub spice mixture
- 2 - Tablespoons vegetable oil
- 1 - Onion halved
- ½ - cup water
- ½ - cup apple cider vinegar
- ½ - cup orange juice
- Slider buns and coleslaw

For the rub:

- 1 - tablespoon brown sugar
- 1 - tablespoon paprika
- 1 - tablespoon ground cumin
- 1 - tablespoon kosher salt
- 1 - teaspoon garlic powder
- 1 - teaspoon black pepper
- ½ - teaspoon cayenne pepper

INSTRUCTIONS

1. Spread the beef rub zest blend all over each floor of the bits of beef undergo, squeezing it into the meat so it sticks.
2. Chicken it is warm, consist of the vegetable oil and dark colored the red meat shoulder portions in bunches, around 3-4mins on each facet, until super darker overlaying
3. On the off hazard that the bottom of the pot begins to consume, consist of extra oil, or upload a bit water to deglaze, scraping up the bits with a wooden spoon.
4. Include the water and undergo a wooden spoon to scratch any sautéed bits
5. Include the apple juice vinegar, squeezed orange, and the pork to the moment pot.
6. Mood killer sauté potential, unfold, and set the load to manual on high for an hour.
7. Fast discharge the weight while the hour is up.
8. Turn the instant pot to sauté via and through. Enable the mixture to stew till it has decreased in volume through about half of.
9. In the period in-between, utilize two forks to dismantle separated the red meat shoulder to wanted floor.

10. Include the beef yet again into the diminished fluid and flip moment pot off.

11. Serve on slider or burger buns with your selected coleslaw, each time wanted.

Nutrition Fact: Calories 199.9g, Fat 6.6g, Carbs 14.2g, Sugars 10.4g, Protein 20.7g

Instant Pot Mexican Beef

Prep Time: 15mins, Cooking Time: 45mins, Servings: 6

INGREDIENTS

- 2½ - Pounds ribs beef brisket
- 1 - Tablespoon chili powder
- 1½ -tsp Crystal kosher salt
- 1 - Tablespoon ghee
- 1 - Medium onion
- 1 - Tablespoon tomato paste
- 6 - Garlic cloves
- ½ - cup roasted tomato salsa
- ½ - cup Instant Pot bone broth
- ½ - tsp Red Boat fish sauce
- Freshly ground black pepper
- ½ - cup minced cilantro
- 2 - Radishes

INSTRUCTIONS

1. The procedure is practically the equivalent paying little heed to whether you utilize a stove-top weight cooker or an electric one.

2. The main contrast is that your cooking time under high weight will be somewhat shorter with the stove top cooker than with an electric cooker.

3. Presses the "Sauté" catch on your Instant Pot and add the ghee to the cooking embed.

4. Chicken the fats dissolved, include the onions and sauté until translucent.

5. Blend in the tomato glue and garlic, and cook for 30 seconds or until fragrant.

6. Toss in the prepared hamburger, and pour in the salsa, stock, and fish sauce.

7. Spread and lock the top, and press the "Keep Warm/Cancel" catch on the Instant Pot.

8. Press the "Manual" or "Weight Cook" catch to change to the weight cooking mode.

9. On the off chance that your blocks are littler than mine, you can press the "less" catch to diminish the cooking time. Chicken the pot is customized, leave.

10. At the point chicken the stew is done the cooking, the Instant Pot will change naturally

11. In case you're utilizing a stove-top weight cooker rather, expel the pot from the warmth. In either case, let the weight discharge normally.

12. Open the top and season to taste with salt and pepper. Now, you can plate and serve.

13. Chicken you're prepared to eat, top the hot stew with cilantro and radishes.

Nutrition Fact: Calories 239g, Fat 7.2g, Carbs 17g, Sugars 8g, Protein 27g

Instant Pot Mocha-Rubbed Pot Roast

Prep Time: 10mins, Cooking Time: 50mins, Servings: 4

INGREDIENTS

For the mocha rub:

- 2 - tsp finely ground coffee
- 2 - tsp smoked paprika
- 1 - tsp ground black pepper
- 1 - tablespoon cocoa powder
- 1 - tsp Aleppo pepper
- 1 - teaspoon chili powder
- 1 - teaspoon ground ginger
- 1 - teaspoon sea salt

For the roast:

- 2 - pounds beef chuck roast
- 1 - cup brewed coffee
- 1 - cup beef broth
- 1 - small onion
- 6 - dried figs
- 3 - tsp balsamic vinegar
- Kosher salt
- Freshly ground black pepper

INSTRUCTIONS

1. Blend the elements for the mocha rub in a little bowl. Blend some espresso.

2. Spot the meat 3D squares in an enormous bowl and add three to four tablespoons of the mocha rub.

3. Toss well until the meat is equally covered.

4. Consolidate the fermented espresso, juices, onion, figs, and balsamic vinegar in a powerful blender. Barrage until melted.

5. Move the prepared meat to your weight cooker and pour the sauce on top.

6. Spread and lock the cover of your weight cooker.

7. In case you're utilizing an Instant Pot, turn it on and press the "Meat/Stew" catch to change it to the weight cooking mode.

8. At the point chicken the stew is done the cooking, the Instant Pot will change consequently to a "Keep Warm" mode.

9. Pop open the top. The meat ought to be fork delicate.

10. Move the cooked meat to a serving platter. Shred the meat with two forks.

11. Chicken ever wanted, heat the rest of the sauce to a bubble to decrease and thicken it. Modify the flavoring with salt and pepper to taste.

12. Scoop the sauce on the meat and delve in!

Nutrition Fact: Calories 293.1g, Fat 7.6g, Carbs 34.8g, Sugars 7.2g, Protein 22.6g

Instant pot Corned Beef and Cabbage

Prep Time: 45mins, Cooking Time: 55mins, Serving: 4-6

INGREDIENTS

- Corned beef brisket
- 3 - cups beef broth
- 4 - bay leaves
- 4 - whole cloves
- 1 - tsp whole white peppercorns
- ½ - tsp mustard seeds
- 2 - drops liquid smoke
- 1 - head green cabbage
- 4 - carrots, cut into bite-sized chunks
- 4 - russet or Yukon gold potatoes

INSTRUCTIONS

1. Add the brisket to the Instant Pot; include the juices, sound leaves, cloves, peppercorns, mustard seeds, and fluid smoke, at that point add enough water to simply almost spread the brisket. Spread and set to "Meat/Stew" under high weight for 55 minutes. Chicken completed, enable it to depressurize normally, around 15 minutes, at that point expel the spread. As it depressurizes, cut up the cabbage, carrots, and potatoes in case you're utilizing them.

2. Move the fluid from the Instant Pot into a stockpot, pouring the fluid through a strainer to get the peppercorns, cloves, and cove leaves. Keep the hamburger in the Instant Pot, spread it, and turn it off; it'll remain warm as we set up the vegetables. Add the carrots and potatoes to the fluid in the stockpot and heat to the point of boiling over drug/high warmth; chicken bubbling, include the cabbage, decrease warmth to low, and spread. Stew until the vegetables are delicate, around 20 minutes, at that point taste and include salt if necessary.

3. Cut the brisket and present with the vegetables and soup.

4. This cooking time will consider delicate meat that is as yet sliceable. In the event that you need it self-destructing, increment the weight cooking time to 65 minutes.

5. Searching for an innovative use for remaining corned meat.

Nutrition Fact: Calories 435g, Fat 12g, Carbs 24g, Sugars 7g, Protein 54g

Instant Pot Taco Meat

Prep Time: 10mins, Cooking Time: 10mins, Serving: 2

INGREDIENTS

- 2 - pounds ground beef
- 4 - tablespoons oil
- 2 - red onions
- 3 - green bell peppers
- 5 - garlic cloves
- 2 - teaspoons chili powder
- 2 - teaspoons oregano
- 1 - teaspoon salt
- 1 - teaspoon dried basil
- ½ - teaspoon turmeric
- ½ - teaspoon black pepper
- 1 - teaspoon paprika
- 1 - teaspoon cumin
- ½ - teaspoon cayenne
- ½ - teaspoon chipotle powder
- Cilantro, garnish

INSTRUCTIONS

1. Press the "sauté" catch and pan-fried food for 5-6 minutes.
2. At that point add the ground meat to the pot and cook until for the most part dark colored.
3. Secure the cover, close the weight valve and cook for 10 minutes at high weight.
4. Normally discharge weight.
5. Open the cover, and on the off chance that the meat discharged any fluid, at that point press the sauté catch to bubble it off.
6. Garnish with cilantro and serve.

Nutrition Fact: Calories 623g, Fat 38g, Carbs 15g, Sugars 6g, Protein 54g

Instant Pot Bolognese Sauce Recipe

Prep Time: 10mins, Cooking Time: 25mins, Serving: 6

INGREDIENTS

- 2 - tablespoons olive oil
- 1 - large brown onion
- 2 - medium carrots
- 2 - celery sticks
- 2 - teaspoons of salt
- ½ - long red chilli
- 2.2 - kg grass-fed ground beef
- 4 - cloves of garlic, diced
- 1 - teaspoon paprika powder
- ½ - teaspoon cinnamon powder
- 1 - teaspoon onion powder
- 2 -tsp Tamari gluten-free soy sauce
- 1 - teaspoon fish sauce
- 2 - bay leaves
- 1 - star anise
- 2 x 400 ml cans organic tomatoes

INSTRUCTIONS

1. Turn the Instant Pot on. Press the Sauté ability key.
2. Include the olive oil, onions, carrots, celery, and bean stew to the pot. Keep the duvet off.
3. Sauté for round 5mins, mixing or multiple instances.
4. Following 5mins include the beef and smash it separated making use of a spatula.
5. Mix through with the greens, at that factor includes the remainder of the fixings apart from the inlet leaf and tomatoes, and blend yet again.
6. Cook on Sauté for 5 additional minutes to darker off the beef.
7. Chicken the beef has modified the shading, include the cleaved tomatoes and blend via.
8. Press Keep Warm/Cancel to stop the sautéing manner.
9. Close and lock the cover of the Instant Pot. Watch that the steam valve take care of is indicating Sealing.
10. Trust that the Instant Pot will blare multiple times to tell you it's getting the possibility to paintings.
11. After round 5 minutes you will see and hear the steam leaving the valve.

12. At the factor chicken time is up, you can deliver the burden a danger to discharge usually or utilize the fast weight discharge approach before beginning the pinnacle. Our Bolognese sauce ought to be thick and bright.

13. On the off risk that you discover that the stew is excessively watery, basically set the Sauté ability back on and cook the sauce discovered for 5-10mins, mixing more than one times.

14. Present with zucchini noodles or your selected pasta, rice or potatoes. Store scraps inside the cooler or cooler.

Nutrition Fact: Calories 354g, Fat 23g, Carbs 52g, Sugars 12g, Protein 73g

Whole30 Instant Pot Thai Beef

Prep Time: 15mins, Cooking Time: 40mins, Servings: 10

INGREDIENTS

- ¼ - cup coconut amino
- 1 - tbsp lime juice
- 2 - tbsp apple cider vinegar
- 2 - tbsp apple juice
- 1 - tbsp Thai Red Curry Paste
- 1 - tbsp Lighthouse Garlic
- 2 - tbsp Lighthouse Cilantro
- 1 - tsp Lighthouse Ginger
- ½ - tsp kosher salt
- 1 - tbsp olive oil
- 2 - jalapenos minced
- 2 - lb beef chuck roast cubed
- 10 - butter lettuce leaves
- 1 - tsp sesame seeds

INSTRUCTIONS

1. In a medium bowl, whisk the coconut amino, lime juice, apple cider vinegar, apple juice, Thai red curry paste, garlic, cilantro, ginger and salt together, set aside.

2. Press the saute button on the Instant Pot, use the adjust button to set on the "normal" setting.

3. Add the olive oil to the Instant Pot, chicken the display says "hot", add the jalapeno, saute 2-3 minutes, add the beef chuck roast and sear for 1-2 minutes.

4. Press the Keep Warm/Cancel button on the Instant Pot.

5. Pour the prepared sauce into the instant pot.

6. Place the lid on the Instant Pot and make sure the steam release is set to "sealing".

7. Press the "manual" button and set the Instant Pot to high pressure, chicken use the +/- buttons to set the Instant Pot to 30 minutes.

8. Chicken the cooking time is up, turn off the Instant Pot and wait 5-10 minutes, chicken release any remaining pressure before unlocking the lid.

9. Remove the lid and use two forks or "meat claws" to shred the beef.

10. Place the beef in the lettuce leaves and sprinkle with sesame seeds.

Nutrition Fact: Calories 543g, Fat 65g, Carbs 42g, Sugars 15g, Protein 84g

Whole30 Instant Pot Ropa Vieja

Prep Time: 10mins, Cooking Time: 1hr, Servings: 5

INGREDIENTS

- 3 - lbs flank steak
- 1 - medium onion
- 1 - green pepper
- 1 - red pepper
- 1 - yellow pepper
- 5 - cloves garlic
- 2 - tsp garlic powder
- 1- tsp dry oregano
- 1 - tsp smoked paprika
- 1 - tsp cumin
- 1 - cup crushed tomatoes
- juice of 1 lime
- 1 - cup compliant olives
- cup ½cilantro
- Salt and Pepper
- jalapeño and avocado
- 2 - tbsp avocado oil

INSTRUCTIONS

1. Set IP to sauté capacity and include avocado oil.

2. Cut flank steak into pieces so it fits in the pot and season the two sides with salt and pepper. Add steak to IP and dark colored the two sides in bunches. Move to plate and set aside.

3. Add onion and peppers to the pot. Sautee 4-5 min or until relaxed. Make sure to scratch any darker bits on the base of the pot. Include garlic and cook another 45-60 sec.

4. Include garlic powder, oregano, paprika, and cumin and toss everything to coat. Sautée 45-60sec to stir the flavors. Include tomatoes, lime juice, and olives. Give everything a blend before adding the steak back to the pot.

5. Spread the steak with the veggies, close the top, set to fixing and cook under high weight 45min.

6. Chicken cooked, discharge weight physically and shred the steak in the pot. Modify salt and pepper as required and include cilantro.

7. Present with caulis rice as well as plantains and topping with jalapeño, avocado, and cilantro

Nutrition Fact: Calories 313g, Fat 7g, Carbs 14g, Sugars 2.4g, Protein 27g

Paleo INSTANT POT MEXI-MEATLOAF

Prep Time: 15mins, Cooking Time: 35mins, Serving: 4

INGREDIENTS

- 2 - pounds ground grass-fed beef
- 1 - cup fire roasted salsa
- 1 - teaspoon cumin
- 1 - teaspoon garlic powder
- 1 - teaspoon chili powder
- 1 - teaspoon paprika
- 1 - teaspoon onion powder
- 1 - teaspoon sea salt
- 1 - tsp ground black pepper
- 1 - large yellow onion
- 1 - pastured egg
- ¼ - cup tapioca starch
- 1 - tablespoon ghee

INSTRUCTIONS

1. Empty some water into the treated steel bowl of your Instant Pot. Presently join all fixings in a bowl, combining great by hand. Structure a portion with your meat blend, squeezing it together immovably. Spoon the 1/4 measure of outstanding flame cooked salsa over your meatloaf. Presently wrap it firmly in foil. Spot the foil wrapped meatloaf on the trivet.

2. Close the top and select the Pressure Cook/Manual catch, utilizing the +/ - catches to change the time until 35 minutes is shown.

3. Guarantee the weight valve is shut and hold up until the cooking time has finished before fast discharging the weight valve. Open the cover chicken safe to do as such and cautiously evacuate your meatloaf. Present with crisp cilantro sprigs and on the off chance that you want a gooey trimming, make sure to sprinkle my QUESO BLANCO sauce for included flavor

Nutrition Fact: Calories 170.8g, Fat 5.5g, Carbs 9.1g, Sugars 1.5g, Protein 21.4g

Instant pot Braised Cubed Steak with Peppers and Olives

Prep Time: 10mins, Cooking Time: 30mins, Serving: 8

INGREDIENTS

- 8 - pieces cubed steak
- 1 ¾ - teaspoons adobo seasoning
- black pepper
- 1 - 8 - oz can tomato sauce
- 1 - cup water
- 1 - small red bell pepper
- ½ - medium onion
- 1/3 - cup green pitted olives

INSTRUCTIONS

1. Season meat with adobo or garlic salt, and dark pepper to taste.
2. Spot into the weight cooker, top with onions and peppers, pour tomato sauce and water over everything and include the olives alongside a portion of the salt water.
3. Spread and cook high weight 25 minutes.
4. Regular discharge and serve

Nutrition Fact: Calories 154g, Fat 5.5g, Carbs 4g, Sugar 1.5g, Protein 23.5g

Instant Pot Beef Stew

Prep Time: 5mins, Cooking Time: 35mins, Serving: 6

INGREDIENTS

- 1 - Tbsp butter or oil
- 2 - pounds beef stew meat
- 3 - cloves garlic
- 2/3 - cup onion
- 2 - medium russet potatoes
- 4 - large carrots
- 1 - cup beef broth
- ¼ - cup tomato paste
- 1 - tsp oregano
- 1.5 - cups frozen peas

INSTRUCTIONS

1. Include the unfold/oil, garlic and meat and dark colored for 3-five minutes.
2. Combine onion, potato, carrots, soup, tomato glue, and oregano and blend to sign up for.

3. Utilize the beef/stew trap to cook.
4. Blend in the cooked peas simply earlier than serving.
5. Serve warm

Nutrition Fact: Calories 310.1g, Fat 14.2g, Carbs 26.3g, Sugars 4.1g, Protein 3.8g

Pot Roast for Instant Pot

Prep Time: 20mins, Cooking Time: 1hr, Serves: 4

INGREDIENTS

- 2-3 - lb chuck roast
- 4 - large carrots
- 4 - medium potatoes
- 1 - large onion
- 2 - cups beef broth
- 1 - tbsp Italian seasoning
- 2 - tsp minced garlic
- 2 - tbsp olive oil
- salt & pepper to taste

INSTRUCTIONS

1. Add the olive oil to the base of the moment pot and turn on the sauté capacity. Salt and pepper and dark colored the two sides of the meal.
2. Chicken the dish has sautéed, expelled from the Instant Pot.
3. Spot the carrots, potatoes, and onion in the base of the Instant Pot.
4. Lay the hamburger cook over the vegetables.
5. Pour the 2 measures of meat stock over the hamburger meat and vegetables.
6. Include additional onion top of the meat broil.
7. Spot the top on the Instant Pot and seal shut.
8. Press manual and set the Instant Pot clock for 60 minutes. Ensure the vent is shut.
9. Let the meal cook and vent normally.
10. Cut the pot broil contrary to what would be expected and present with vegetables and the in its natural juices left in the Instant Pot.

Nutrition Fact: Calories 309.4g, Fat 15g, Carbs 11.1g, Sugars 2g, Protein 32.1g

One Pan Tuscan Pork Loin

Prep Time: 25mins, Cooking Time: 15mins, Serving: 6

INGREDIENTS

- 1 ¼ - lbs Pork Loin
- 1 - large onion

- 8 - cloves garlic
- 8 - oz cherry tomatoes
- 1 - lemon sliced thin

INSTRUCTIONS

1. Preheat stove to 450 degrees.
2. Warmth overwhelming dish on the stove on medium high.
3. Include pork midsection, dark colored all sides.
4. Include onions, sauté with pork until daintily seared.
5. Include tomatoes, garlic, and lemon-heat on high until tomatoes pop.
6. Move to the stove and cook until pork's inner temperature achieves 140-155 degrees.
7. Let sit, shrouded in a skillet, for at any rate 8 minutes. This will enable pork's interior temperature to raise another 5 degrees and let the juices set.
8. Cut and serve. Plate with tomatoes, onions, and garlic from dish

Nutrition Fact: Calories 144g, Fat 1g, Carbs 4g, Sugar 1g, Protein 21g

Prosciutto Wrapped Pork Tenderloin

Prep Time: 10mins, Cooking Time: 40mins, Servings: 4

INGREDIENTS

- 1 – 2 - pound Pork Tenderloin
- 2 - oz of Prosciutto
- ¼ - cup honey omit if Paleo
- ¼ - cup dijon mustard
- salt and pepper

INSTRUCTIONS

1. Preheat stove to 400 degrees
2. In little bowl consolidate nectar and dijon
3. Spread out Prosciutto on material, somewhat covering.
4. Spot pork on Prosciutto.
5. Brush with nectar dijon blend and sprinkle with salt and pepper.
6. Lifting material, move up.
7. Prepare for 30-40 minutes or until meat thermometer peruses 160 degrees for medium well.
8. Let rest 10 minutes before cutting

Nutrition Facts: Calories 355g, Fat 12g, Carbs 18g, Sugars 17g, Protein 40g

Instant Pot Banana French Toast

Prep Time: 15mins, Cooking Time: 30mins, Servings: 6

INGREDIENTS

- 6 - slices french bread
- 4 - bananas sliced
- 2 - tablespoons brown sugar
- ¼ - cup cream cheese
- 3 - eggs
- ¼ - cup milk
- 1 - tablespoon white sugar
- 1 - teaspoon vanilla extract
- ½ - teaspoon ground cinnamon
- 2 - tablespoons butter
- ¼ - cup pecans chopped
- Pure maple syrup optional

INSTRUCTIONS

1. Oil a half QT round making ready dish or cake look for gold 8 qt Instant Pot. In the event which you have a bit weight cooking pot, make use of a heating dish so that it will in shape within the pot.
2. Layer one reduce banana over the bread, at that point sprinkle one tablespoon of darker sugar over the bananas.
3. In a microwave, soften the cream cheddar 30-forty five seconds till it is velvety enough to unfold.
4. Include the rest of the bread to the bowl and layer one progressively reduce banana over the bread.
5. Sprinkle one tablespoon of darkish-colored sugar over the bananas and 1/2 of the walnuts over the pinnacle.
6. Spot reduce margarine portions over the bread because the pinnacle layer.
7. In a blending bowl, beat the eggs with a whisk. Whisk milk, white sugar, vanilla, and cinnamon into egg combo.
8. Pour egg combo over the bread, making a point to coat the bread properly.
9. In the occasion that you don't have a trivet to raise the work out of the new weight cooker, make a sling out of an sizable foil strip.
10. Focus the dish on the trivet or foil strip and decrease it into the burden cooker.
11. Lock the duvet installation. Select High Pressure and set the clock for 25mins.
12. On the off chance that using an Instant Pot, select the porridge catch, at that factor upload five minutes to the cooking time.

13. At the point while the clock is going off, flip off the weight cooker and turn the steam discharge valve to "venting" to discharge the burden.

14. Keep French toast dish in weight cooker to heat for 5mins before evacuating pinnacle.

15. Let set for a further five minutes, at that point top with reduce bananas, nuts and maple syrup earlier than serving.

Nutrition Fact: Calories 377.2g, Fat 10.7g, Carbs 59.1g, Sugars 7.2g, Protein 15.6g

INSTANT POT POULTRY RECIPES

Instant Pot Salsa Chicken with Cauliflower Rice

Prep Time: 5mins, Cooking Time: 9mins, Serves: 4

INGREDIENTS

Salsa Chicken:

- 4 - boneless skinless chicken breasts
- 16 - oz of salsa
- ½ - cup chicken broth
- salt & pepper

Cauliflower:

- Cauliflower Rice Ingredients
- 1 - large head cauliflower
- 3 - tablespoons olive oil
- salt to taste

INSTRUCTIONS

1. Spot the chicken bosoms in the base of the Instant Pot and season with salt and pepper to flavor.
2. Pour the salsa and water or fowl inventory over the chicken bosoms.
3. Spot the quilt at the Instant Pot and seal shut.
4. Press manual and set the clock to 9 minutes.
5. Enable the Instant Pot to vent usually.
6. In the interim, make the cauliflower rice on the stovetop.
7. Cauliflower Rice
8. Trim the cauliflower florets, getting rid of but a great deal stem as can be anticipated.
9. In three bunches, upload the florets to a sustenance processor or Vitamix and heartbeat till the blend looks as if rice.
10. Blend in cauliflower and season with salt.
11. Cook, mixing an awful lot of the time till the cauliflower has mollified three to 5mins.
12. Shred the chook and serve over rice cauliflower.

Nutrition Fact: Calories 412.7g, Fat 27.4g, Carbs 18.1g, Sugars 3.9g, Protein 25.6g

Paleo Instant Pot Butter Chicken

Prep Time: 5mins, Cooking Time: 10mins, Servings: 5

INGREDIENTS

- 4 - tbsp ghee clarified butter
- 10 - garlic cloves
- 1 - tbsp fresh ginger root
- 2 to 3 large shallots
- 2 - lbs chicken thighs
- 28 - oz. roasted tomatoes
- ¼ - cup full fat coconut milk
- Cilantro
- Salt and pepper
- 1 - tbsp garam masala powder
- 2 - tsp smoked paprika
- 1.5 tsp coriander powder
- 2 - tsp turmeric powder

INSTRUCTIONS

1. Moment Pot: Press Sauté capacity - include 2 tbsp ghee. At the point chicken the oil is liquefied, include slashed garlic, ginger, and shallots. Season with squeeze of salt. Sauté until fragrant. Include Dry Spice Seasonings. Give a speedy sauté to marginally heat up the flavors.

2. Include 2 jars of flame cooked tomato and scratch the base of the pot to guarantee that nothing is adhering to the base. Include chicken and spread the sauce over every piece. Seal the cover and valve. Press Manual - 10 minutes. Chickenever done, regular discharge until the valve drops.

3. Scoop out the chicken. Include ¼ container full-fat coconut milk and 2 tbsp ghee. Puree the sauce utilizing a submersion blender until rich smooth. * Dice the chicken to nibble sizes and add them back to the sauce pot. Give it a mix and topping with slashed cilantro. Serve the margarine chicken over marginally cooked cauliflower rice or pureed potatoes.

Nutrition Fact: Calories 329g, Fat 23g, Carbs 10g, Sugar 3g, Protein 21g

Instant Pot Chicken Tikka Masala

Prep Time: 10mins, Cooking Time: 10mins, Servings: 6

INGREDIENTS

- 1 –tablespoon butter ghee
- 2 –tablespoons coconut oil
- 1 -large onion

- 1 – tablespoon garam masala
- 2 –teaspoons salt
- 1 –teaspoon cumin
- 1 –teaspoon turmeric
- 1 –teaspoon ground coriander
- 1 –teaspoon chili powder
- ½ -teaspoon ground pepper
- 6 - 7 –cloves garlic
- 2 - knob of ginger
- 124 oz can organic tomatoes
- 2- ½ pounds chicken breasts
- 3 –tsp yogurt coconut milk
- 2 –tablespoons almond
- ½ -cup bone broth

INSTRUCTIONS

1. Press the Sauté to catch on the Instant Pot and include the margarine or ghee and coconut oil to soften.
2. Include the diced onion and sauté 3 to 5 minutes.
3. Include the flavors and blend, cooking around 1 minute, until fragrant.
4. At that point include garlic, ginger, squashed tomatoes, and 1/2 glass juices.
5. Spot the cubed chicken bosom into the Instant Pot, submerging it under the tomato-zest blend.
6. Lock the top, ensure the vent is fixed, and press the Manual catch. Alter the opportunity to 10 minutes.
7. At the point chicken the Instant Pot signals, discharge the weight right away.
8. Utilizing an opened spoon, expel the chicken pieces from the sauce, place into a bowl, and put aside.
9. Mix in the almond or cashew margarine and yogurt.
10. Utilizing an inundation blender, mix the tomato sauce until smooth and thick.
11. Return the chicken to the mixed sauce and serve

Nutrition Fact: Calories 207.5g, Fat 14.3g, Carbs 4.8g, Sugars 2.3g, Protein 17.2g

Instant Pot Garlic Lemon Chicken

Prep Time: 15mins, Cooking Time: 15mins, Serving: 4

INGREDIENTS

- 1–2 - pounds chicken breasts
- 1 - teaspoon sea salt

- 1 - onion, diced
- 1 - tablespoon avocado oil, lard
- 5 - garlic cloves
- ½ - cup organic chicken broth
- 1 - teaspoon dried parsley
- ¼ - teaspoon paprika
- ¼ - cup white cooking wine
- 1 - large lemon juiced
- 3–4 - teaspoons arrowroot flour

INSTRUCTIONS

1. Turn your Instant Pot onto the sauté issue and see within the diced onion and cooking fat
2. Cook the onions for five-10 minutes or until diminished. You can likewise cook dinner till they begin to dark colored
3. Include the relaxation of the fixings except the arrowroot flour and relaxed the cover for your Instant Pot
4. Permit prepare dinner time to complete, discharge steam valve to vent and after that cautiously evacuate pinnacle
5. Now you may thicken your sauce via creating slurry.
6. To try this evacuate round 1/4 container sauce from the pot, include the arrowroot flour, and after that reintroduce the slurry into the staying fluid
7. Blend and serve right now. This likewise warms properly as scraps

Nutrition Fact: Calories 467.7g, Fat 23.3g, Carbs 30.6g, Sugars 2.8g, Protein 36.6g

Instant Pot Curried Lemon Coconut Chicken

Prep Time: 5mins, Cooking Time: 35mins, Serving: 6

INGREDIENTS

- 1 - can full fat coconut milk
- ¼ - c. lemon juice
- 1 - Tbs. curry powder
- 1 - tsp. turmeric
- ½ - tsp. salt
- about 4 lbs. chicken
- ½ -1 tsp. lemon zest

INSTRUCTIONS

1. Blend the coconut milk, lemon squeeze and flavors together in a bowl or glass estimating container.

2. Pour a tad on the base of the Instant Pot.

3. Include the fowl.

4. Pour within the relaxation, along with the coconut cream piece at the off threat which you have one, over the chicken.

5. Lock inside the top and near the valve.

6. Turn the IP to "rooster" which must be 15 minutes at excessive weight.

7. In the event that operating with solidified chicken bosoms, add 10mins to the prepare dinner time and you need to be exceptional.

8. It will take round 20mins to get the opportunity to weight.

9. After the 15 second cooks time, make use of the rapid discharge by beginning the valve.

10. Test chicken for doneness by means of slicing open and looking the middle.

11. Utilize 2 forks to shred the chook up in the pot.

12. Present with steamed or cooked veggies or over rice.

Nutrition Fact: Calories 335.8g, Fat 12.1g, Carbs 28.7g, Sugars 7.9g, Protein 27.1g

Instant pot Chicken Cacciatore

Prep Time: 20mins, Cooking Time: 25mins, Serving:

INGREDIENTS

- Extra Virgin Olive Oil
- 3 - Shallots
- 4 - Garlic Cloves
- 1 - Green Bell Pepper
- ½ - cup brand Organic Chicken
- 8-10 - oz package mushrooms
- 5-6 - Skinless Chicken Breasts
- 2 - Cans Organic Tomatoes
- 2 - Tb Organic Tomato Paste
- 1 - Can Pitted Black Olives
- Fresh Parsley
- Red Pepper to taste
- Sea Salt & Black Pepper

INSTRUCTIONS

1. Warmth the oil in a 4-quart or bigger cooker. Include the shallots and ringer pepper and cook over medium-high warmth, blending every now and again, until the shallots mellow marginally, around 2 minutes

2. Mix in the stock and bubble for 2-3 minutes. Scrape up any caramelized bits adhering to the base of the cooker.

3. Blend in the mushrooms and garlic. Set the chicken on top. Spread the chicken with squashed tomatoes. Try not to blend. Thud the tomato glue on top.

4. Lock the top set up.

5. Over high warmth bring to high weight.

6. Diminish the warmth only enough to keep up high weight and cook for 8 minutes.

7. Mood killer the warmth.

8. Enable the strain to descend normally. Expel the top.

9. Blend in the olives, parsley, red pepper pieces, salt and pepper.

Nutrition Fact: Calories 423g, Fat 35.3g, Carbs 5.2g, Sugars 1.2g, Protein 21.3g

Instant pot Lemon Olive Chicken

Prep Time: 15mins, Cooking Time: 10mins, Serving: 4

INGREDIENTS

- 4 - Boneless Skinless Chicken Breasts
- ½ - teaspoon organic cumin
- 1 - teaspoon Sea Salt
- ¼ - teaspoon Black Pepper
- ½ - cup Organic Grass-Fed Butter
- 1 - lemons 1/2 juiced
- 1 - cup Chicken Bone Broth
- 1 - can pitted green olives
- ½ - cup Red onion

INSTRUCTIONS

1. Generously season chicken bosoms with ocean salt, cumin and dark pepper

2. Set your multi cooker to sauté and darker chicken bosoms in margarine on the two sides.

3. Include every outstanding fixing and bring to a stew.

4. Spread your multi cooker with the cover and cook under strain for 10 minutes. At the point chicken done weight cooking, utilize the speedy weight discharge technique.

Nutrition Fact: Calories 438g, Fat 21g, Carbs 27g, Sugars 3.2g, Protein 71g

Instant pot Summer Italian Chicken

Prep Time: 5mins, Cooking Time: 15mins, Servings: 6

INGREDIENTS

- 8 - boneless chicken thighs
- Diamond Crystal kosher salt
- 1 - tsp ghee avocado oil
- 1 - small onion
- 2 - medium carrots
- ½ - pound cremini mushrooms
- 3 - garlic cloves
- 1 - tablespoon tomato paste
- 2 - cups cherry tomatoes
- ½ - cup pitted green olives
- ¼ - tsp cracked black pepper
- ½ - cup fresh basil leaves
- ¼ - cup Italian parsley

INSTRUCTIONS

1. Get your chook thighs and sprinkle ¾ teaspoons healthy salt throughout them.
2. Press the "Sauté" seizes on the Instant Pot or warmth a stovetop weight cooker over medium warmth. Include your fat of selection.
3. At the point while the fats are sparkling, encompass the onions, carrots, and mushrooms, and a ½ teaspoon legitimate salt.
4. Mix inside the garlic and tomato glue, and cook for round 30 seconds or until aromatic.
5. Include the salted fowl, cherry tomatoes and green olives to the pot.
6. Mood killer the sauté potential, and lock the quilt at the weight cooker.
7. In case you're utilizing an Instant Pot, press the "Manual" or "Weight Cook" seize and set the cooking time to 7 minutes for chook bosoms and 10mins for thighs.
8. At the point while the chook is completed cooking, turn on the stovetop fumes fan earlier than turning the load cooker valve to discharge the steam.
9. Expel the pinnacle right away to avert overcooking. Include the newly damaged dark pepper and exchange the flavoring with extra salt as required.
10. In the occasion which you want a thicker sauce, evacuate the chook and mix up the veggies and cooking fluid with a drenching blender.
11. Blend inside the new herbs, and serve right away.
12. Toss any scraps within the fridge for as long as four days or in the cooler for so long as a 1/2 year.

Nutrition Fact: Calories 323g, Fat 53g, Carbs 22g, Sugars 12g, Protein 73g

Braised Chicken Drumsticks in Tomatillo Sauce

Prep Time: 35mins, Cooking Time: 25mins, Serving: 6

INGREDIENTS

- 6 - chicken drumsticks
- 1 - tbsp cider vinegar
- 1 - tsp kosher salt
- 1/8 - tsp black pepper
- 1 - teaspoon dried oregano
- 1 - teaspoon olive oil
- 1 ½ - cups jarred tomatillo sauce
- ¼ - cup chopped cilantro
- 1 - jalapeno

INSTRUCTIONS

1. Season chook with vinegar, salt, pepper, and oregano. Marinate multiple hours if time presents.
2. Set the Instant Pot to sauté; while warm encompass the oil and the chicken to darker on the 2 sides, round 4mins on every aspect.
3. Include the tomatillo salsa, 2 tablespoons of the cilantro and jalapeno, unfold and prepare dinner on excessive weight 20 minutes, till the chicken is delicate.
4. At the factor whilst the load discharges, adorn with cilantro and serve over rice each time wanted.

Nutrition Fact: Calories 161g, Fat 5g, Carbs 5g, Sugar 2g, Protein 22g

Whole Roasted Chicken with Lemon & Rosemary

Prep Time: 40mins, Cooking Time: 30mins, Serving: 4

INGREDIENTS

- 1 - whole chicken
- 1 - tsp fresh rosemary
- 1 ½ –2 tablespoons olive oil
- 4–6 - cloves garlic
- ½ - teaspoon paprika
- 1 - teaspoon kosher salt
- ¼ - teaspoon black pepper
- zest from 1 lemon
- 1 - cup chicken broth
- 1 - large onion

INSTRUCTIONS

1. Evacuate anything within fowl. Tenderly wash whole winged creature with virus water and pat dry with paper towels. Spot in heating container or platter and put aside.
2. Preheat electric weight cooker to sauté mode, or begin warming stove-top weight cooker on the stove top.
3. In a little bowl consolidate rosemary, olive oil, garlic, paprika, salt, pepper, and lemon get-up-and-go. In the wake of zesting, cut lemon down the middle and stuff in the depression of chicken. Spread zest blend all over the winged creature, rubbing onto all sides.
4. Sprinkle some olive oil in your hot dish and spot chicken bosom side down into the pot. Leave for 3-4 minutes, until brilliant dark colored. Flip chicken over and rehash for the opposite side.
5. Expel chicken from skillet and set back onto platter or preparing dish where it was previously. Add juices to container and utilize a spatula to scratch off seared bits from skillet.
6. Cook on high weight for 6 minutes for each pound. At the point chicken time is up, let rest for 10 minutes before discharging steam. Evacuate chicken and spot on cutting board rose with foil for at any rate 5 minutes before cutting.
7. Chicken ever wanted, separate squeezes in container and make sauce.

Nutrition Fact: Calories 335.8g, Fat 12.1g, Carbs 28.7g, Sugars 7.9g, Protein 27.1g

Instant Pot Butter Chicken

Prep Time: 15mins, Cooking Time: 17mins, Serving: 2-3

INGREDIENTS

- 2–3 - lbs boneless chicken thighs
- 1 - Tbsp ghee
- 1 ½ - large onions
- 2 ½ - – 3 1/3 tsp salt
- 2 - tsp garlic powder
- 2 - tsp ginger powder
- 2 - heaping tsp turmeric
- 2 - heaping tsp paprika
- 1 ½ - tsp cayenne powder
- 1 ½ - – 2 cups stewed
- 370 - ml tomato paste
- 2 400ml cans coconut milk
- 2 - heaping tsp garam masala
- ½ - cup sliced almond
- ½ - cup cilantro

INSTRUCTIONS

1. In the event that your weight cooker has a sauté setting, use it to liquefy ghee.
2. Include 2 tsp salt and onions. Cook until onions are delicate and translucent
3. Include garlic, ginger, turmeric, paprika and cayenne. Blend in and cook until fragrant.
4. Include canned tomatoes and the watery part of coconut milk, blending completely with flavors.
5. Include chicken and blend well.
6. Expecting you've chosen to utilize nibble measured bits of chicken, an opportunity to cook the chicken will be quick: 8-10 minutes relying upon the weight your cooker employments. With the Instant Pot it took 8 minutes of pressurized cooking time on the Manual-High mode.
7. Chicken cooked, utilize the brisk arrival of weight, blend in coconut cream, tomato glue, garam masala and the vast majority of the cilantro. Include progressively salt if necessary.
8. Top with cut almonds and trimming with more cilantro.

Nutrition Fact: Calories 423g, Fat 35.3g, Carbs 5.2g, Sugars 1.2g, Protein 21.3g

Instant Pot Chicken Pho

Prep Time: 30mins, Cooking Time: 1hr, Servings: 4

INGREDIENTS

For the broth:

- 1 - tablespoon coriander seeds
- 3 - whole cloves
- 2 - inch fresh ginger
- 1 - large yellow onion
- 7 - cups water
- 4 - lb whole chicken no bigger
- 1 - small Fuji apple
- ¾ - cup coarsely cilantro sprigs
- 1 - tablespoon Diamond Crystal kosher salt
- Red Boat fish sauce
- 1 - 2 - teaspoons maple syrup

For the bowls:

- 4 - medium zucchini spiralized
- ½ - small yellow onion
- 2 - green onions green
- ¼ - cup cilantro leafy

- Thai basil leaves optional

INSTRUCTIONS

1. Toss the coriander seeds and cloves in a 6-quart weight cooker. Press the sauté trap on Instant Pot and toast the flavors for a few minutes, shaking or blending, until fragrant. Toss within the ginger and onion and mix the whole lot till aromatic, 45 to 60 seconds.

2. Pour in 4 bins (1 l) of the water to forestall the cooking manner. Cautiously vicinity the chicken inside the cooker, bosom aspect up.

3. Include the apple, cilantro, salt, and ultimate three mugs (0.71 l) water.

4. Press the Cancel/Keep Warm catch, lock the quilt installation, and make certain the valve on pinnacle is within the fixed position. Press the Manual catch and set the Instant Pot to cook dinner below excessive weight (~12 psi) for 14 minutes.

5. Chicken ever completed, flip off the Instant Pot and let the burden decline normally for 20 minutes. Set a clock and if the weight hasn't definitely discharged whilst it dings, turn the valve on the top to hastily vent the rest of the weight. Evacuate the quilt, tilting it a long way from you to evade the hot steam.

6. Hold up a further 5mins earlier than utilizing tongs to transport the chook to an considerable bowl; if components tumble off in travel, do not stress. Add cold water to cover the fowl and drench for 10 minutes to chill and counteract drying. Pour off the water, incompletely spread, and put the chicken apart to chill.

7. Skim some fat from the soup, earlier than stressing it via a Chinois or muslin-covered work strainer situated over a giant pot. Dispose of the solids. You should finish up with around 7 boxes stock.

8. In the case of using right away, season the soup with the fish sauce, extra salt, and possibly a smidge of the maple syrup. Or alternatively, somewhat unfold the unseasoned inventory and permit cool, at that point refrigerate for as long as 3 days or stop for so long as three months; heat and season before utilizing.

9. Utilize a blade or your hands to isolate the bosom meat and legs from the chicken. Put apart 50% of the chicken for every other usage. Hold the staying fowl for pho bowl accumulating. The chook can be refrigerated for so long as 3 days or solidified for as long as 3 months; carry to room temperature to utilize.

10. Prep and amass the dishes. Cut or shred the chicken into chomp size portions. Dispose of the pores and skin or spare it for cracklings. Carry the soup to a stew over medium warm temperature as you're accumulating the dishes.

11. Separation the zucchini noodles among 4 soup bowls. Top the zoodles with destroyed fowl.

12. Check the juices season over again, increase the warm temperature, and warmth it to the factor of boiling. Spoon around 2 mugs (480 ml) inventory into each bowl.

13. At that point beautify with onion, inexperienced onion, cilantro, basil, pepper, and sriracha every time wanted. You can weigh down on new lime juice, as properly. Serve right away!

Nutrition Fact: Calories 412.7g, Fat 27.4g, Carbs 18.1g, Sugars 3.9g, Protein 25.6g

Instant Pot Sweet Potato Chicken Curry

Prep Time: 15mins, Cooking Time: 20mins, Serving: 4-5

INGREDIENTS

- 2 - tsp. ghee or coconut oil
- ½ - medium yellow onion
- 3 - garlic cloves
- 1 - lb chicken breast
- 1 - sweet potato
- 1 - red pepper
- 2/3 - cup chicken broth
- 3 - Tbsp. curry powder
- 1 - tsp. cumin
- 1 - tsp. ground turmeric
- ½ - tsp. cayenne
- ½ - tsp. sea salt
- 14 - oz. full fat coconut milk
- 2 - cups frozen green beans
- Cashews, cilantro

INSTRUCTIONS

1. Set your Instant pot to the sauté putting.
2. Include the ghee, onion, and garlic and sauté till onions are translucent.
3. At that point visit guide putting and set temp to excessive.
4. Include the chicken, sweet potatoes, pink pepper, soup, curry, cumin, turmeric, cayenne and ocean salt.
5. Chicken time is up, discharge the weight by means of converting from seal to vent.
6. Chicken weight is discharged, expel top and turn Instant Pot to sauté placing.
7. Mix in the coconut milk and solidified and allow prepare dinner for an extra 2-three minute or till the green beans are warmed through.
8. In the meantime, sauté cauliflower rice in a skillet on medium warm temperature with 1-2 tsp. Of ghee.
9. Period of time to sauté cauliflower rice will depend upon within the event that it is in a crisp or solidified state.

Nutrition Fact: Calories 308.9g, Fat 1.4g, Carbs 36.1g, Sugars 4.4g, Protein 33g

Instant Pot Lemon and Garlic Chicken

Prep Time: 25mins, Cooking Time: 20mins, Serving: 6

INGREDIENTS

- 4 - tbsp ghee, 3 - tbsp of olive oil
- 5-6 - cloves of crushed garlic
- juice and zest of 1 lemon
- ¼ - tsp pepper, ½ - tsp salt
- 1 - tsp seasoning of choice
- 2 - lbs of boneless chicken thighs
- 1 - lb red potatoes, 1 - lb green beans
- ½ - cup chicken stock, rice

INSTRUCTIONS

1. First, soften 3-4 tbsp of ghee or spread and blend with 3 tbsp of olive oil.
2. Include 5-6 cloves of squashed garlic, squeeze, and pizzazz of 1 lemon, ¼ tsp pepper, ½ tsp salt, and 1 tsp flavoring if decision next sauté your chicken thighs or bosoms, add lemon and garlic blend to chicken and include potatoes and green beans.
3. On the off chance that cooking in moment pot includes ½ glass chicken juices. Cook for 15-20mins in moment pot and 3-4 hours on high in moment pot.
4. Present with caulis rice or rice of decision.

Nutrition Fact: Calories 205.3g, Fat 5.8g, Carbs 1.1g, Sugars 0.3g, Protein 35.1g

Instant Pot Chicken Cacciatore

Prep Time: 10mins, Cooking Time: 35mins, Serving: 4

INGREDIENTS

- 4 - chicken thighs
- kosher salt and fresh pepper
- olive oil spray
- ½ - can, 14 oz crushed tomatoes
- ½ - cup diced onion
- ¼ - cup diced red bell pepper
- ½ - cup diced green bell pepper
- ½ - teaspoon dried oregano
- 1 - bay leaf
- 2 - tablespoons chopped basil

INSTRUCTIONS

1. Press saute on the Instant Pot, lightly shower with oil and dark colored chicken on the 2 aspects a couple of minutes. Put aside.
2. Shower with incredibly extra oil and include onions and peppers.
3. Sauté until mellow and outstanding, five minutes.
4. Pour tomatoes over the chicken and vegetables, consisting of oregano, narrows leaf, salt, and pepper, provide it a brisk blend and unfold.
5. Cook high weight 25mins; ordinary discharge.
6. Evacuate straight leaf, decorate with parsley and serve over pasta, squash or whatever you want

Nutrition Fact: Calories 133g, Fat 3g, Carbs 10.5g, Sugar 5g, Protein 14g

Instant Pot Chicken Tikka Masala

Prep Time: 5mins, Cooking Time: 25mins, Servings: 6

INGREDIENTS

- 2 - lbs boneless chicken breast
- 1 - small onion
- ½ - yellow bell pepper
- 2 - tablespoons butter
- 1 - teaspoon cumin
- 1 - teaspoon coriander
- 2 - teaspoons garam masala
- 1 - teaspoon turmeric
- ¼ - teaspoon cayenne pepper
- 1 ½ - teaspoon sea salt
- 15 - oz can diced tomatoes
- ½ - cup full fat coconut milk
- 3 - cloves garlic, minced
- 1 - teaspoon grated fresh ginger

INSTRUCTIONS

1. Set your Instant Pot to Sauté. Include unfold, onion, and yellow peppers and cook dinner for 3-4mins until vegetables start to diminish.
2. Include garlic, ginger, flavors, and salt and cook dinner for an extra 1-2 minutes.
3. Include tomatoes and coconut milk and blend properly to enroll in.
4. Spot chicken over combination. Close the pinnacle and set to Poultry.
5. At the point chicken the cycle is finished, evacuate chook and shred. Utilizing a submersion hand blender, puree the sauce.

6. Add the chicken back to the sauce and regulate flavoring to taste.

Nutrition Fact: Calories 280g, Fat 13g, Carbs 6g, Sugar 2g, Protein 33g

Instant Pot Chicken Burrito Bowls

Prep Time: 20mins, Cooking Time: 10mins, Serving: 6

INGREDIENTS

- 1 - cup prepared salsa
- 1 - pound chicken breasts
- ½ - teaspoon ground cumin
- Salt and pepper
- ½ - head cauliflower

Topping Ideas:

- shredded lettuce
- chopped tomatoes
- green onions
- shredded cheese
- black beans

INSTRUCTIONS

1. Sprinkle a half teaspoon of cumin, similarly to salt and pepper over the pinnacle, but don't combination.
2. Spot a 2. Five-inch trivet over the fowl, at that point positioned a broiler-safe bowl this is 7-crawls in width similarly.
3. Empty the cauliflower florets into the bowl.
4. Secure the pinnacle to the Instant Pot the move the steam discharge valve to Sealing.
5. At the factor while the cooking cycle is completed, let the load generally discharge for 10mins earlier than transferring the steam discharge valve to Vent.
6. At the factor while the skimming valve drops, to flag that the burden has been discharged, you could securely evacuate the top.
7. Use broiler gloves to expel the bowl of cooked cauliflower and the trivet, at that point use tongs to move the cooked chicken to a reducing board to rest for a couple of minutes.
8. It would not need to be impeccable - that is a "rural" style cauliflower rice.
9. Season the rice to flavor with quite salt and pepper.
10. Utilize forks to shred the chicken on the reducing board, at that point move it lower back to the salsa inside the Instant Pot and provide it a combination to coat nicely.
11. Remains may be positioned away in remote sealed shut holders inside the ice chest for so long as 3 days.
12. The remaining chook makes an extraordinary serving of mixed veggies topper.

Nutrition Fact: Calories 293.4g, Fat 6.6g, Carbs 40.6g, Sugars 3.3g, Protein 19g

Instant Pot Chicken and Mushroom

Prep Time: 5mins, Cooking Time: 30mins, Serving: 6

INGREDIENTS

- 2 - tablespoons avocado oil
- 1 - large onion
- 2 - cloves garlic
- 1 - bay leaf
- 2 - cups sliced baby bella
- 2 - sprigs rosemary
- 2 - pounds chicken thighs
- 2 - teaspoons fine salt
- 1 - teaspoon ground black pepper
- 1 - teaspoon garlic powder
- ½ - teaspoon ground nutmeg
- 2 - tablespoons red wine vinegar
- ½ - cup coconut cream
- 1 - scoop Vital Proteins gelatin

INSTRUCTIONS

1. Warmth your weight cooker on sauce mode.
2. Include the avocado oil, onion, garlic, and sound leaf. Sauté for 8-10 minutes until delicate. Include the mushrooms and rosemary. Sauté for an additional 5 minutes until caramelized and delicate.
3. Include the chicken thighs and flavoring. Sauté, mixing once in a while until the chicken is generally seared. At that point include the vinegar and blend, rejecting up any flavoring that adhered to the base of the container.
4. Include a ¼ measure of cream. Drop the sauté work, close the top and set to weight cook on high for 10 minutes.
5. At the point chicken it's set, discharge the weight physically. Open the cover and set to decrease or sauté until it goes to a stew.
6. Mix, destroying the chicken with tongs or forks. Decrease the fluid considerably, at that point mix in the rest of the cream and gelatin until smooth.
7. Move the chicken and sauce to a serving bowl. Give it a chance to cool for 5-10 minutes before serving; the sauce will get additional rich in this time.

Nutrition Fact: Calories 263g, Fat 15g, Carbs 2g, Sugar 0.2g, Protein 30g

Instant Pot Sweet and Sour Chicken

Prep Time: 10mins, Cooking Time: 20mins, Servings: 6

INGREDIENTS

- 1.5 - lbs chicken thighs
- Sea salt and pepper
- 2 - Tbsp coconut oil
- 1 20 oz can pineapple chunks
- 1 ½ - cups pineapple chunks
- ¾ - pineapple juice
- 1/3 - cup apple cider vinegar
- 1/3 - cup Whole30 ketchup
- 4 - cloves garlic minced
- 1 - inch fresh ginger
- 1 - large red bell pepper
- 1/8 - tsp red pepper flakes
- 1 ½ - Tbsp arrowroot starch
- Green onions for garnish
- Sesame seeds for garnish

INSTRUCTIONS

1. Have your fixings cut/slashed and prepared to utilize. Turn your moment pot to "sauté" and once it peruses "HOT" include the coconut oil. Sprinkle your chicken with a touch of salt and pepper while trusting that pot will warm.

2. Include chicken and cook around 1-2 minutes on each side, turning with tongs. Try not to cook the chicken through or sit tight for it to turn darker - burning it on the two sides is the objective.

3. While chicken sautés, whisk together the 1/2 container pineapple juice, vinegar, ketchup garlic, ginger, and red pepper drops.

4. After chicken sautés, and include the sauce blend, pineapple lumps, and red Chile pepper, and bring to a stew. Drop sautes capacity. Secure the cover, place the steam discharge on "fixing" and set to high weight for 5 minutes

5. Following 5 minutes, speedy discharge the weight by turning steam discharge to "venting". Chicken weight is discharged, cautiously expel the cover.

6. In a little bowl, whisk together the arrowroot starch with outstanding 1/4 container pineapple juice until broke down, at that point add to the pot and cautiously mix.

7. Press "drop" and enable the pot to chill off a bit before serving. Serve hot, embellished with cut green onions and toasted sesame seeds, nearby cauliflower rice and additionally cooked broccoli.

Nutrition Fact: Calories 290g, Fat 9g, Carbs 28g, Sugar: 22g, Protein: 23g

Instant Pot Honey Mustard Chicken

Prep Time: 5mins, Cooking Time: 25mins, Servings: 6

INGREDIENTS

Chicken:

- 2 - lbs chicken thighs
- 4 - cloves garlic minced
- Sea salt and black pepper
- 2 - Tbsp ghee
- Chopped parley for garnish

Sauce:

- 2 - Tbsp coconut amino
- 2¼ - tbsp. chicken bone broth
- 3 - Tbsp raw honey melted
- ¼ - cup spicy brown mustard
- 1 ½ - Tbsp fresh lemon juice

To Thicken Sauce:

- 1 - tsp arrowroot starch
- 2 - Tbsp bone broth

INSTRUCTIONS

1. Whisk together all sauce fixings in a bowl until smooth, put aside

2. Turn your Instant Pot to "sauté" and enable it to warm in the interim, sprinkle chicken with ocean salt and dark pepper on the two sides.

3. After pot peruses "hot", twirl ghee around the base to give it a chance to warm. It's imperative to include the ghee AFTER the pot warms to keep the chicken from staying

4. Include chicken, skin side down, and cook until brilliant darker at that point flip chicken with tongs and rehash on the second side.

5. At the point chicken the two sides are brilliant dark colored, sprinkle garlic around the chicken and enable it to cook around 30-45 seconds, until mollified, at that point press "drop".

6. Pour sauce blend over the chicken, secure the cover, place steam discharge to "fixing" and set on high weight for 10mins.

7. Chicken time is up, fast discharge the weight and expels cover. Utilizing tongs expel chicken to a plate and put aside while you thicken the sauce.

8. Drop the weight cook, press "sauté" and whisk together the 2 Tbsp stock and arrowroot, at that point add to sauce and mix. Cook around 3-5 additional minutes or until sauce is thickened to inclination. Return chicken to pot with its juices and coat with sauce.

Nutrition Fact: Calories 378g, Fat 26g, Carbs 12g, Sugar 8g, Protein 22g

INSTANT POT FISH AND SEAFOOD RECIPES

Shrimp Stir Fry Paleo, Whole30 & Low Carb

Prep Time: 15mins, Cooking Time: 25mins, Serving: 5

INGREDIENTS

- 1 - pound shrimp
- 2 - zucchini
- 1 - green pepper
- 1 - cup sugar snap peas
- 1 - cup shredded carrots
- ½ - red onion
- ½ - cup green onion
- 1/3 - cup chicken
- 1/3 - cup coconut amino
- 3 - tsp olive oil, divided
- 1 - tablespoon minced garlic
- ½ - tablespoon minced ginger
- 1 - tsp dried parsley
- 1/8 - teaspoon salt
- 1/8 - teaspoon pepper

INSTRUCTIONS

1. In a significant skillet over medium warm temperature, consist of 1 tablespoon olive oil, ginger and garlic
2. Chicken fragrant, include shrimp, salt, pepper and parsley and cook 4 minutes on each facet, or till cooked totally
3. While shrimp is cooking, be a part of soup, coconut amino and meat gelatin in a little bowl and placed aside
4. Expel shrimp from skillet and put apart
5. Permit to cook dinner, blending plenty of the time, till fork sensitive/delicate
6. Expel from the skillet and placed aside for stressing out the overabundance water
7. Dispose of the general public of the overabundance water from the skillet and see lower back on stovetop over medium warmth
8. Include closing 1 tablespoon of oil to the dish and include the crimson and green onion, pepper, carrots and sugar snap peas, mixing at times
9. Cook for six-8mins, or until vegetables are fork delicate and sparkling

10. While the greens are cooking, enclose zucchini noodles by a paper towel to wring out or utilize a nut milk % to expel any overabundance water
11. Include sauce into the dish with the greens, blending to consolidate
12. At that point include shrimp and zucchini noodles returned in and cook dinner for 2mins, blending every sometimes to coat shrimp and zucchini
13. Expel from warmth, the sauce will thicken because it cools
14. Top with sesame seeds, parsley, and additional inexperienced onion
15. Serve and admire

Nutrition Fact: Calories 293.4g, Fat 6.6g, Carbs 40.6g, Sugars 3.3g, Protein 19g

Buttery Oven Roasted Shrimp

Prep Time: 2mins, Cooking Time: 8mins, Serving: 6

INGREDIENTS

- 2 - Pounds Wild Caught Deveined Shrimp
- Olive Oil
- Salt/Pepper
- ½ - Cup Butter - melted
- Juice of 1 Large Lemon
- 2 - teaspoons Worcestershire Sauce
- Salt-Free Cajun Seasoning

INSTRUCTIONS

1. Preheat stove to 400°F
2. Wash defrosted shrimp in virus water and channel absolutely.
3. In a large bowl, toss shrimp with a liberal sprinkle of olive oil till equally blanketed.
4. Move shrimp to good sized rimmed making ready sheet.
5. Blend dissolved spread, lemon juice, and Worcestershire sauce. Pour combination over shrimp.
6. Sprinkle with cajun flavoring.
7. Heat for six-8 minutes or until shrimp is pink and marginally twisted.
8. Top with crisp parsley and serve.

Nutrition Fact: Calories 291.1g, Fat 16.3g, Carbs 4.5g, Sugars 0.6g, Protein 30g

Whole30 Keto Blackened Salmon with Cajun Zoodles

Prep Time: 15mins, Cooking Time: 15mins, Servings: 2

INGREDIENTS

- 3 or 4 medium-size zucchini
- ½ -teaspoon salt

- 1 -red bell pepper
- 2 –cloves garlic crushed
- 4 –tablespoons butter
- ½ to ¾ -lb wild caught salmon
- ½ -teaspoon salt
- Cajun seasoning

INSTRUCTIONS

1. Initially, incapacitate the zucchini to make noodles, or "zoodles".
2. Set the zoodles on a towel and sprinkle with half teaspoon of salt.
3. Finely cube the ringer pepper and placed apart.
4. Daintily sprinkle salt on one facet of the salmon filets. At that point liberally shake Cajun flavoring over the salt.
5. Turn the salmon over, and rehash the primary salt, at that point Cajun flavoring.
6. Dissolve 2 tablespoons spread or ghee in a solid iron skillet on a medium-excessive warm temperature.
7. Flip the fish over and prepare dinner 2 or 3mins longer.
8. Try not to strain over washing the skillet; you are going to make use of it over again!
9. Include the more 2 tablespoons unfold or ghee to the skillet, at that point the diced ringer pepper. Cook 2mins.
10. Chicken you've pressed all of the water you can out of the zoodles, upload it to the skillet with the ringer pepper and mix to consolidate.

Nutrition Fact: Calories 212.1g, Fat 12.3g, Carbs 0.5g, Sugars 2g, Protein 23.9g

Salmon Burgers

Prep Time: 15mins, Cooking Time: 20mins, Serving: 4

INGREDIENTS

Salmon Burgers:

- 12 - oz. wild-caught salmon
- ½ - lemon, juiced
- 1 - small shallot
- 2 - green onions
- 1 - Tbsp. fresh dill
- 2 - tsp. Dijon mustard
- ¼ - tsp. salt
- ¼ - tsp. pepper
- 2 - eggs
- ¼ - cup almond flour

- 1 - Tbsp. coconut oil

For the Avocado Garlic Sauce:

- 1 - medium avocado
- ¼ - cup extra virgin olive oil
- ½ - lemon, juiced
- 1 - tsp. Dijon mustard
- 1 - Tbsp. fresh dill
- 2 - garlic cloves
- ¼ - tsp. salt
- 1/8 - tsp. pepper

INSTRUCTIONS

1. Consolidate the majority of the salmon burger fixings, with the exception of the coconut oil, in a huge bowl and blend well. On the off chance that blend is truly wet, include extra almond flour 1 Tbsp. at once.
2. Structure into 6-8 patties. Patties effectively self-destruct until they are cooked. Handle with alert.
3. Warmth coconut oil on a frying pan or dish to medium-high warmth.
4. Chicken hot, cautiously add burgers to the skillet and cook for 5-6 minutes on each side or until cooked through. Patties should sizzle chicken added to the skillet.
5. To serve, top with 1-2 Tbsp. avocado garlic sauce and fold into a lettuce wrap in the event that you wish.
6. For the Avocado Garlic Sauce:
7. In a sustenance processor or blender, consolidate the majority of the fixings and procedure until smooth.

Nutrition Fact: Calories 195g, Fat 9g, Carbs 4g, Sugar 1g, Protein: 24g

Spaghetti Squash Shrimp Scampi

Prep Time: 10mins, Cooking Time: 30mins, Serving: 4

INGREDIENTS

For the Spaghetti Squash:

- 1 - spaghetti squash
- 1–2 - tablespoons olive oil
- ½ - teaspoon pepper
- ½ - teaspoon salt
- 2 - tablespoons water

For the Shrimp:

- 1 - pound peeled shrimp

- 4 - tablespoons ghee
- 2 - tablespoons minced garlic
- 1 - tsp extra virgin avocado oil
- ½ - teaspoon salt
- ½ - teaspoon pepper
- ½ - teaspoon red pepper flakes
- ½ - teaspoon dried basil
- ½ - teaspoon dried oregano
- ½ - lemon

INSTRUCTIONS

For the squash:

1. Utilize one of these strategies to cook spaghetti squash
2. Expel the strings, spread to keep warm and put aside

For the Shrimp:

3. While spaghetti squash is cooking:
4. Include ghee, additional virgin olive oil and minced garlic to sauté dish over medium warmth
5. Let join for a couple of minutes, until garlic is fragrant. Include shrimp
6. Include the remainder of the flavors, blend to join
7. Give shrimp and sauce a chance to stew for around 5 minutes or until shrimp is cooked
8. Include shrimp and sauce and a press of lemon to squash noodles
9. Present with another crush of crisp lemon on and new parsley on top

Nutrition Fact: Calories 161.6g, Fat 3.5g, Carbs 8.4g, Sugars 4.3g, Protein 22.1g

15 Minute Chili Lime Shrimp

Prep Time: 15mins, Cooking Time: 15mins, Serving: 4-6

INGREDIENTS

- 1 - pound defrosted
- ¼ - cup lime juice
- 2 - tablespoons olive oil
- 2 - teaspoons chili powder
- 1 - teaspoon garlic powder
- ½ - teaspoon salt
- 1 - handful of cilantros

INSTRUCTIONS

1. In a vast bowl or zip lock baggie, join shrimp and all fixings apart from cleaved cilantro

2. Blend well to equitably coat and permit marinate for 15 minutes

3. In the occasion that flame broiling, add shrimp to sticks and barbeque for 4 minutes on each aspect and expel from the warmth

4. In the event that sautéing, consist of the substance of bowl into a big non-stick skillet over medium warm temperature

5. Cook for 4mins on each aspect and expel from the warmth

6. Enhancement with cilantro

7. Serve and appreciate

Nutrition Fact: Calories 309.5g, Fat 8g, Carbs 8.2g, Sugars 2.2g, Protein 45.4g

Grilled Salmon Cucumber Salad

Prep Time: 5mins, Cooking Time: 10mins, Servings: 2

INGREDIENTS

- 1 - tbsp olive oil extra virgin
- 1 - Atlantic salmon fillet around 0.42 kg
- 2 - tbsp seafood seasoning blend
- 2 - cups cucumber chopped
- 1 - cup cherry tomatoes chopped
- ½ - red onion chopped
- dash salt and pepper
- 1 tbsp olive oil extra virgin

INSTRUCTIONS

1. Expel skin and wash the salmon filet. Cut salmon into 2-4 pieces and spot in a skillet over medium warmth.

2. Sprinkle olive oil and a portion of the fish flavoring over the filets. Cook for 4 minutes for every side, flipping and sprinkling the remainder of the flavoring on the opposite side. Include hacked cucumber, cherry tomatoes, and red onion to a huge serving of mixed greens bowl. Include salt, pepper, and olive oil and prepare the plate of mixed greens together.

3. Cut the salmon into strips and spot over the plate of mixed greens, partition as wanted. Appreciate

Nutrition Fact: Calories 112.5g, Fat 1g, Carbs 0.9g, Sugars 0.2g, Protein 20.4g

Paleo Zucchini Pasta with Spicy Shrimp Marinara

Prep Time: 15mins, Cooking Time: 15mins, Servings: 2 -4

INGREDIENTS

- 3 - small-med zucchinis
- 8 - oz shrimp

- generous pinch sea salt
- ¼ - tsp smoked paprika
- 1 - tbsp cooking fat of choice
- 1-15 oz can organic
- 1-2 - tbsp olive oil
- 2 - cloves garlic
- 2 - tsp Italian seasoning blend
- ¼ - cup chopped fresh basil
- ½ - tsp salt or to taste
- ¼ - tsp crushed red pepper

INSTRUCTIONS

1. Put your spiral zed zucchini in a great bowl constant with a paper towel and sprinkle with a large squeeze of ocean salt, placed aside.
2. Add the tomatoes, Italian flavoring, and squashed red pepper and salt, blend and warmth till genuinely effervescent.
3. Turn the warm temperature all the way down to low, include the new basil, and permit to tenderly stew.
4. While the sauce stews, heat a sizeable skillet over medicinal drugs howdy warmth and include your cooking fats.
5. Sprinkle the shrimp with a liberal squeeze of ocean salt and the smoked paprika, at that factor upload to the hot skillet.
6. Cook 2-three minutes on each side till softly caramelized outwardly and cooked via.
7. Warmth a comparable skillet certainly over drug greetings warmth.
8. Ensure the zucchini noodles are depleted of overabundance water and upload them to the skillet, mixing and cooking for round 2-3 minutes, till definitely mollified.
9. Try now not to overcook they get an increasing number of watery the greater they're cooked for.
10. Expel sauce from the warmth and toss with the zucchini pasta in a serving bowl.
11. Topping with additional new basil every time wanted, and serve heat. Appreciate

Nutrition Fact: Calories 207.2g, Fat 10.2g, Carbs 6g, Sugars 3g, Protein 23.7g

Whole30 Bang Bang Shrimp

Prep Time: 10mins, Cooking Time: 10mins, Servings: 4

INGREDIENTS

Shrimp:

- 1 - pound shrimp
- 1 - egg whisked well
- 2/3 - cup coconut flour

- ½ - cup arrowroot powder
- ½ - teaspoon salt
- pepper to taste
- Avocado oil for frying
- Green onions green part only
- sesame seeds for garnish

Bang Bang Sauce:

- 2¼ - Tbsp. mayonnaise
- 2 ½ - tsp. sriracha or hot sauce
- 2 ¼ - Tbsp. ketchup
- 1 ½ - tsp. coconut amino
- 1 - garlic clove
- salt to taste

INSTRUCTIONS

1. Mix together regardless of sauce fixings and set.
2. Whisk together coconut flour, arrowroot powder, salt, and pepper in a wide bowl. Dunk shrimp in eggs at that point dig in flour. Shake off overabundance and spot on a preparing sheet or plate. Rehash with all shrimp.
3. Warmth a meager layer of oil in a huge skillet over medium warmth. Working in clumps, sear shrimp, making a point not to swarm. Hold up until the base side is pleasantly sautéed before flipping, at that point flip and cook through on the opposite side. Shrimp ought to be perfectly seared and firm. Expel from skillet with an opened spoon and rehash until all shrimp are seared.
4. In a huge bowl, toss shrimp with half of the sauce. Add more sauce to taste and toss. Present with outstanding sauce. Top with cut green onions and sesame seeds.

Nutrition Fact: Calories 269g, Fat 8.2g, Carbs 35.1g, Sugars 12g, Protein 16.2g

Creamy Lemon Shrimp Paleo Summer Sauce

Prep Time: 5mins, Cooking Time: 10mins, Serving: 4

INGREDIENTS

- 1 - pound shrimp
- 2/3 - cup Original flavored nut pods
- 1/3 - cup water or broth
- 1 - tablespoon arrowroot starch
- 1 - tablespoon olive oil
- 1 - tablespoon minced garlic
- 1 - teaspoon salt
- 1 - teaspoon pepper

- Juice of 1 lemon
- Lemon and parsley to garnish

INSTRUCTIONS

1. Warmth oil and garlic in an enormous skillet over medium warmth
2. Chicken skillet is hot and garlic is fragrant, place shrimp in a solitary layer
3. Juice 1 lemon over shrimp and season with salt and pepper
4. Chicken shrimp are nearly cooked all together, include nut pods and water or juices and lower heat a bit
5. Blend to consolidate the fluids
6. Move shrimp to the sides of the container to make a vacant territory in the focal point of the skillet
7. Gradually include the arrowroot starch while speeding until broken up and no clusters remain
8. Whisk/blend the shrimp and sauce together
9. Expel from warmth, decorate with lemon and parsley and serve right away

Nutrition Fact: Calories 193.6g, Fat 6g, Carbs 13.2g, Sugars 5.1g, Protein 22.4g

Buffalo Shrimp Spaghetti Squash and Paleo Ranch Dressing

Prep Time: 15mins, Cooking Time: 35mins, Servings: 4

INGREDIENTS

- 2 - small spaghetti squash
- 16 - oz shrimp
- 2 - TBSP clarified butter or ghee
- 1 - tsp paprika
- salt and pepper to taste
- ¼ - cup Frank's Red-Hot sauce
- ¼ - small red onion sliced thin
- 2 - 3 - TBSP fresh herbs

Paleo ranch dressing

- ¼ - cup quality store bought
- ½ - cup canned coconut milk
- ½ - tsp garlic powder
- ½ - tsp dried dill
- ½ - tsp sea salt
- ½ - tsp parsley fresh or dried

- ¼ - tsp onion powder
- ¼ - tsp black peper
- dash of hot sauce

INSTRUCTIONS

1. Pre-heat range to 400 tiers F.
2. Cut the stemmed part off your spaghetti squash at that point cuts down the middle longwise and scoop out the seeds. Rehash for each squash.
3. Next clutch a lipped making ready sheet. Rub the reduce facet of the squash with olive oil or spread and spot to your heating sheet and dish face-down for round half-hour, or until delicate and efficiently penetrated with a fork.
4. While the squash cooks, prep your dressing + shrimp.
5. For the dressing, be a part of all fixings in a bricklayer container and shake nicely. A spot in an ice chest to kick back. The dressing may be made ahead of time and delighted in for approx. 4 days.
6. Clean and strip shrimp, defrost if important. Recently we have been shopping solidified, deveined, easy strip shrimp. I should simply defrost, strip, and prepare dinner.
7. Warmth a huge container or skillet to medium-high warms with 2 TBSP of unfold and sauté your shrimp. Season with paprika, salt, and dark pepper to flavor. Cook on each aspect for around 2mins till shrimp twist and become misty.
8. Add your hot sauce to the dish and mix to coat even as the shrimp are as yet warm.
9. Chicken squash is ready, allow to chill, at that point cushion the spaghetti-like strands with a fork. Keep them in the squash bowls or bit the strands out on plates! You might also season the squash with salt + pepper inside the occasion which you'd like.
10. Add your wild ox sauced shrimp to every squash vessel and bathe the relaxation of the sauce over every. Top with red onion and a sprinkling of crisp herbs.
11. Present with farm dressing and extra warm sauce for sprinkling.

Nutrition Fact: Calories 460g, Fat 27.7g, Carbs 9.7g, Sugars 0.6g, Protein 41.9g

Skillet Tilapia with Tomatoes

Prep Time: 15mins, Cooking Time: 10mins, Serving: 3

INGREDIENTS

- 3 - pieces of tilapia
- 2 ½ - tbsp olive oil
- 2 - cups grape
- salt and pepper
- parsley or basil for garnish

INSTRUCTIONS

1. Warmth a skillet over medium-high warm temperature and encompass 1 tbsp olive oil.
2. Sprinkle fish with salt and pepper.

3. Add to a box and sauté for around 3mins for every facet or till fish is cooked through.
4. Evacuate to a plate and spread with foil.
5. Include half tbsp olive oil to box and tomatoes. Salt and pepper to taste.
6. Cook for round 4mins or till they make a few darkish colored and start to rankle, tossing at times.
7. Add fish returned to a similar dish and warm for a moment.
8. Serve proper away.

Nutrition Fact: Calories 116g, Fat 9g, Carbs 6g, Sugar 2g, Protein 1g

Shrimp and Kielbasa Skillet

Prep Time: 5mins, Cooking Time: 15mins, Serving: 4

INGREDIENTS

- 1 - pound shrimp
- ½ - kielbasa sausage link
- ½ - green pepper
- ½ - red pepper
- ½ - onion
- 1 - zucchini or summer squash
- ½ - cup chicken stock
- 2 - tablespoons avocado oil
- 1 - tablespoon Old Bay seasoning
- 1/8 - teaspoon salt
- 1/8 - teaspoon pepper
- 1/8 - teaspoon red pepper flakes
- 1 - teaspoon tapioca flour/starch
- ½ - cup Nutpods Original
- Parsley or cilantro to garnish

INSTRUCTIONS

1. Warmth skillet over medium warmth with 1 tablespoon olive oil
2. Include shrimp and 2 teaspoons Old Bay flavoring
3. Cook for 2 minutes until murky. Expel from skillet and put aside
4. Include 1 tablespoon oil, onions, and pepper to skillet
5. Cook 4 minutes until they begin to relax
6. Include zucchini, kielbasa, salt, pepper, and red pepper pieces. Cook for 4-5 minutes
7. Include shrimp back in with the chicken stock. Bring to a stew
8. Permit to stew for 2 minutes, mixing every so often

9. Move meat and veggies to the side, making a little open space on the skillet
10. Include Nut pods or almond milk with the custard starch
11. Utilize a fork to consolidate together until starch isn't clumpy
12. Mix into meat and veggies with outstanding 2 teaspoons of Old Bay flavoring, giving it a pleasant rich consistency
13. Expel from warmth, trimming and serve

Nutrition Fact: Calories 520.4g, Fat 34.2g, Carbs 11.4g, Sugars 2.5g, Protein 40.6g

Whole30 Sheet Pan Fish Fajitas

Prep Time: 10mins, Cooking Time: 20mins, Serving: 4

INGREDIENTS

- 1 - pound cod
- 3 - bell peppers
- 1 - large white onion
- 1 - lime, juiced
- 2 - tablespoons avocado oil
- 1 - tablespoon minced garlic
- 2 - teaspoons chili powder
- 1 - teaspoon cumin
- 1 - teaspoon dried parsley
- 1 - teaspoon chipotle powder
- ½ - teaspoon coriander
- ½ - teaspoon onion powder
- ½ - teaspoon salt
- ¼ - teaspoon pepper

INSTRUCTIONS

1. Preheat stove to 400 degrees F.
2. Line a sheet dish with tin foil
3. In a medium bowl, combine dried seasonings and put aside
4. Spot onions and peppers onto sheet dish and shower 2 tablespoons oil, minced garlic and juice from 1/2 of the lime
5. Use hands to combine on the sheet skillet, covered with oil, garlic and lime juice
6. Sprinkle 1/2 of the flavoring blend over veggies on the sheet dish
7. Use hands to equally coat veggies with flavoring blend and spread out uniformly on the sheet container
8. Spot into the stove and prepare for 12 minutes

9. While veggies are preparing, place cod pieces into the bowl with the rest of the flavoring blend

10. Include 1 tablespoon oil and squeeze of outstanding 1/2 lime

11. Use hands to uniformly coat fish with seasonings, oil, and lime. Rub flavoring into the fish well

12. Expel sheet skillet from the broiler, mix veggies and spot fish onto the sheet dish

13. Set back into the stove and heat for 10-12mins until fish effectively chips with a fork

14. Expel from stove, serve over cauliflower rice or tacos and appreciate

Nutrition Fact: Calories 123.6g, Fat 6.4g, Carbs 2.7g, Sugars 1.2g, Protein 12.4g

Whole30 thai seafood coconut soup

Prep Time: 15mins. Cooking Time: 20mins, Serves: 4

INGREDIENTS

- 2–14 --ounce cans full fat coconut milk
- 2 - cups low-sodium chicken broth
- 1 - tablespoon fish sauce
- 1 – jalapeno, 2 - limes
- ¾ - pound shrimp, 1 - pound haddock filet
- 2 – zucchini, 1 - carrot
- ¼ - cup chopped basil

INSTRUCTIONS

1. Get-up-and-go one lime and cut down the middle. Put aside. Spiralize zucchini with the littlest sharp edge putting and put aside.

2. Warmth a Dutch stove or profound, huge stockpot over medium-high warmth. Include coconut milk and chicken soup and heat to the point of boiling, mixing. Include carrots, fish sauce, and lime pizzazz and crush the juice from the zested lime into the soup, mixing.

3. Lessen warmth to medium-low. Include haddock and mix delicately. Let stew for around 3-4 minutes, until fish is nearly done. Include shrimp and mix delicately. Enable soup to stew for around 2-3 minutes more until fish is cooked through.

4. Drop a home of zucchini noodles in the focal point of four huge soup bowls. Spoon soup over the noodles and let represent roughly 2-3 minutes with the goal that zucchini can relax a bit. Cut the second lime into wedges and topping with cilantro. Serve right away.

Nutrition Fact: Calories 372.8g, Fat 23.3g, Carbs 18.5g, Sugars 3.2g, Protein 29.1g

Sheet Pan Lemon Garlic Salmon and Veggies

Prep Time: 10mins, Cooking Time: 40mins, Serving: 4

INGREDIENTS

- 4 - salmon fillets
- 2 - pounds red potatoes
- ½ - pound green beans
- ½ - lemon
- 3 - tablespoons avocado
- 1–2 - tablespoons minced garlic
- ¾ - teaspoons black pepper
- ¼ - teaspoon salt

INSTRUCTIONS

1. Preheat the broiler to four hundred ranges F.
2. Slash the potatoes into equal size 3-d squares
3. On a preparing sheet, use palms to coat the potatoes with 2 tablespoons oil, pepper, and minced garlic
4. Organize the potatoes in a solitary layer and see in the stove
5. Prepare for 30 minutes till fork sensitive
6. Before it is completed preparing, trim the closures off the green beans and coat with 1/2 tablespoon oil and salt
7. Expel potatoes from the broiler, flip and add inexperienced beans to the sheet container and include a press of lemon squeeze over sheet dish
8. Either move potatoes and inexperienced been to the perimeters and notice salmon inside the inside or location over the top
9. Spot lemon cuts on sheet field or legitimately on the salmon
10. Put the sheet box once more into the range and cook for around 10mins, till salmon is effectively chipped with a fork
11. Serve and recognize

Nutrition Fact: Calories 123.6g, Fat 6.4g, Carbs 2.7g, Sugars 1.2g, Protein 12.4g

Whole30 Cedar Plank Orange Glazed Salmon

Prep Time: 30mins, Cooking Time: 25mins, Serving: 4-6

INGREDIENTS

- 1.5 - pound salmon filet
- ½ - cup orange juice
- 1 - tablespoon melted ghee
- 4 - tablespoons coconut amino

- 2 - tablespoons honey
- 1 - teaspoon garlic powder
- ¼ - teaspoon salt
- ¼ - teaspoon pepper
- ½ - orange, sliced

INSTRUCTIONS

1. Absorb cedar board water half-hour preceding flame broiling. Warmth flame broil to 500 ranges
2. Join squeezed orange, ghee, coconut amino, nectar, garlic powder, salt and pepper in a bit bowl
3. With a meat brush, brush combination onto the salmon and allow marinate at the same time as the cedar board is splashing.
4. Chicken cedar board has doused and flame broil is warmed, place cedar board on the fish fry till there may be a blackout smell of smoke, round 3-4mins.
5. Spot salmon at the cedar board, brush with coating all over again, pinnacle with greater orange cuts and spread the flame broil
6. Let prepare dinner for 10 minutes. Have the relaxation of the coating, seasoning brush and splash bottle with water beneficial near the barbecue.
7. Following 10mins, open the flame broil, brush with first-rate coating.

Nutrition Fact: Calories 240.2g, Fat 12.4g, Carbs 7.4g, Sugars 3.4g, Protein 24.6g

Creamy Skillet Salmon

Prep Time: 5mins, Cooking Time: 15mins, Serving: 4

INGREDIENTS

- 4 - skinless salmon fillets
- 2/3 - cup heavy cream replacement
- 1 - cup halved cherry tomatoes
- 1 - large handful arugula
- 2 - tablespoons olive oil
- 2 - tablespoons ghee
- 2 - tablespoons minced garlic
- 1 - tablespoon arrowroot flour
- ½ - teaspoon salt
- ¼ - teaspoon pepper

INSTRUCTIONS

1. Warmth oil in a huge skillet and add salmon filets to container
2. Cook 5 minutes on each side and expel from dish

3. Include milk, garlic, ghee, salt and pepper
4. Chicken hot, gradually rush in arrowroot flour
5. Include tomatoes and arugula
6. Keep mixing for 2 minutes while sauce thickens and vegetables shrink
7. Include salmon once again into the dish and let warm
8. Spread with sauce, expel from warmth and serve

Nutrition Fact: Calories 240.2g, Fat 12.4g, Carbs 7.4g, Sugars 3.4g, Protein 24.6g

Whole30 Sheet Pan Fish Fajitas

Prep Time: 10mins, Cooking Time: 20mins, Serving: 4

INGREDIENTS

- 1 - pound cod
- 3 - bell peppers
- 1 - large white onion
- 1 - lime, juiced
- 2 - tablespoons avocado oil
- 1 - tablespoon minced garlic
- 2 - teaspoons chili powder
- 1 - teaspoon cumin
- 1 - teaspoon dried parsley
- 1 - teaspoon chipotle powder
- ½ - teaspoon coriander
- ½ - teaspoon onion powder
- ½ - teaspoon salt
- ¼ - teaspoon pepper

INSTRUCTIONS

1. Preheat broiler to 400 degrees F. Line a sheet skillet with tin foil
2. In a medium bowl, combine dried seasonings and put aside
3. Spot onions and peppers onto sheet skillet and sprinkle 2 tablespoons oil, minced garlic, and juice from 1/2 of the lime
4. Use hands to combine on the sheet container, equally covered with oil, garlic and lime juice
5. Sprinkle 1/2 of the flavoring blend over veggies on the sheet skillet
6. Use hands to equitably coat veggies with flavoring blend and spread out uniformly on the sheet skillet
7. Spot into the stove and prepare for 12 minutes

8. While veggies are preparing, place cod pieces into the bowl with the rest of the flavoring

9. Include 1 tablespoon oil and squeeze of outstanding 1/2 lime

10. Use hands to uniformly coat fish with seasonings, oil, and lime.

11. Expel sheet container from the broiler, blend veggies and spot fish onto the sheet dish

12. Set back into the stove and prepare an extra 10-12 minutes until fish effectively pieces with a fork

13. Expel from stove, serve over cauliflower rice or tacos and appreciate

Nutrition Fact: Calories 301.4g, Fat 17.6g, Carbs 6.9g, Sugars 3g, Protein 30.2g

Paleo Fish Tacos with Mango Salsa

Prep Time: 15mins, Cooking Time: 10mins, Serving: 3-4

INGREDIENTS

For the Tacos:

- 8 - grain-free tortillas
- 1 - pound halibut or cod
- 1 - cup coconut oil
- 1 - egg, beaten
- ½ - cup shredded purple cabbage
- ½ - cup tapioca flour
- ¼ - cup coconut flour
- 1 - teaspoon garlic powder
- ½ - teaspoon salt
- ½ - sliced jalapeño
- ½ - cup diced cilantro
- Microgreens
- Sliced avocado

For the Mango Salsa:

- 2 - mangos
- ½ - cup red onion
- ¼ - cup cilantro
- ½ - jalapeño
- ½ - teaspoon salt
- Juice of 1 lime

INSTRUCTIONS

1. Shakers fish into 1-inch pieces

2. Consolidate coconut flour, custard flour, garlic powder, and salt into a little bowl beside the bowl with the beaten egg

3. Warmth coconut oil in a huge skillet over medium-high warmth

4. While the coconut oil comes warms up, plunge fish into the egg, at that point straightforwardly into flour blend and equally coat

5. At the point chicken coconut oil is hot, use thongs to include fish pieces into the skillet

6. Cook 1-2 minutes until brilliant dark colored on the principal side

7. Flip each bit of fish and cook another 1-2 minutes until fish is cooked through

8. Expel fish from the warmth and let sit on a plate fixed with a paper towel to assimilate any overabundance oil

9. Include fish, garnishes and mango salsa to the tortillas and appreciate

Nutrition Fact: Calories 254g, Fat 9.4g, Carbs 19g, Sugars 4g, Protein 57g

Instant pot fish shakshuka with cauliflower rice

Prep Time: 10mins, Cooking Time: 15mins, Servings: 2

INGREDIENTS

For the Shakshuka:

- ½ - Tbsp Avocado oil
- ½ - Large Red pepper
- 1 ½ - tsp Taco Seasoning
- 1–14 - oz Can diced tomatoes
- 2/3 - Cup Salsa
- 1 - Tbsp Tomato paste
- 4 - Large eggs
- Salt and Pepper
- ½ - Large avocado
- Cilantro, for garnish
- Sliced green onion, for garnish

For the cauliflower rice:

- 3 - Cups Cauliflower
- 1 ½ - tsp Avocado oil
- 1/3 - Cup Cilantro
- Fresh lime juice
- Salt and pepper

INSTRUCTIONS

1. Warmth the avocado oil up in an enormous, high-sided skillet on medium/high warmth. Include the cut red pepper and cook until it starts to mollify around 2-3 minutes.
2. Include the taco flavoring and cook until fragrant, around 1 minute. Include the jar of diced tomatoes, the salsa, and the tomato glue. Heat to the point of boiling.
3. Chicken bubbling, lessen the warmth to medium and stew until the sauce starts to decrease, around 7-8 minutes.
4. While the sauce stews, place the cauliflower in a sustenance processor and procedure until separated and rice-like.
5. Warmth the extra oil in a medium dish over medium-high warmth, and cook the cauliflower until softly brilliant dark colored, blending sometimes. Chicken cooked, move to a bubble and blend in the cilantro. Season with a crush of new lime squeeze and salt and pepper to taste. Spread to keep warm.

6. Chicken the sauce has diminished, split the 4 eggs into the skillet, leaving room in the middle of them. Sprinkle each with salt and pepper and spread the skillet with a cover. Cook until the eggs are done just as you would prefer.

7. Partition the cauliflower rices between 2 bowls, trailed by the shakshuka, and after that the cut avocado.

8. Embellishment with somewhat more cilantro and the green onion and season to taste with salt and pepper.

Nutrition Fact: Calories 543g, Fat 24g, Carbs 17g, Sugars 4g, Protein 64g

Whole30 Meatless Buffalo Burgers

Prep Time: 10mins, Cooking Time: 35mins, Serving: 8-9

INGREDIENTS

- 4 - cups riced cauliflower
- ½ - cup cooked, mashed sweet potato
- 2 - eggs
- 3 - tablespoons buffalo sauce
- ½ - cup finely diced yellow onion
- 1 - cup + 2 tbsp almond flour
- ½ - teaspoon salt

INSTRUCTIONS

1. Preheat broiler to 375

2. Join the uncooked, riced cauliflower with the pounded sweet potato, eggs, wild ox sauce, yellow onion, almond flour, and salt. Blend well to join the squashed sweet potato equally

3. Line a heating sheet with material paper and scoop out about 1/2 measure of the meatless burger blend. Delicately form into a patty around 1-inch thick at that point place on the preparing sheet – the blend will be extremely wet, so maneuver carefully. Patties can likewise be smoothed in the wake of setting on the material paper

4. Spot heating sheet into the broiler and prepare for 35-40 minutes, until patties are cooked all through and hold together

5. Discretionary: For a marginally fresh top, keep the patties in the stove and turn the grill on high. Sear for 4 minutes – watch the burgers so they don't consume

Nutrition Fact: Calories 240.2g, Fat 12.4g, Carbs 7.4g, Sugars 3.4g, Protein 24.6g

Cheesy" Paleo Broccoli Casserole

Prep Time: 10mins, Cooking Time: 15mins, Serving: 12

INGREDIENTS

- 2 - lbs broccoli florets
- 1 - tbsp coconut oil
- 1 - onion chopped
- 4 - garlic cloves minced
- Parsley flakes for garnish

"Cheese" Sauce

- 1 ½ - cup full-fat coconut milk
- 1 - cup raw cashews
- ¾ - cup nutritional yeast
- 1/3 - cup apple cider vinegar
- 2 - tbsp dijon mustard
- 1 - tsp onion powder
- 2 - tsp sea salt
- ½ - tsp ground black pepper
- ½ - tsp smoked paprika
- 2 - eggs

INSTRUCTIONS

1. Preheat stove to 350 degrees F.
2. Spot broccoli in a 9x13 preparing dish in an even layer.
3. Warmth 1 tbsp of coconut oil a skillet over medium high warmth.
4. Include onion and garlic and cook blending until fragrant, around 5 minutes.
5. Expel from warmth and add to the preparing dish over the broccoli.
6. In a blender, include all elements for the "cheddar" sauce, with the exception of eggs, and mix until smooth and velvety.
7. Heartbeat in the eggs until simply combined.
8. Pour over the vegetables and mix together.
9. Prepare for 1 hour until brilliant.
10. Sprinkle with parsley chips and serve warm.

Nutrition Facts: Calories 176g, Fat 13g, Carbs 11g, Sugars 2g, Protein 6g

Butternut Squash Broccoli Kale Salad

Prep Time: 10mins, Cooking Time: 20mins, Servings: 4

INGREDIENTS

- 1 - head broccoli
- 3 - cups cubed butternut squash
- 1 - red onion
- 1 - bulb garlic
- 1 ½ - tbsp olive oil
- ½ - tsp salt
- 1 - bunch Tuscan Kale
- 1/3 - cup olive oil
- 2 - tbsp balsamic vinegar
- 1 - egg yolk
- ½ - tsp black pepper
- 1/3 - cup almonds

INSTRUCTIONS

1. Preheat the stove to 220 degrees Celsius. Spot the cubed butternut squash, broccoli florets and red onion on a preparing plate. Cut the top off of the garlic bulb and spot it on the heating plate. Shower everything with 1/2tbsp olive oil and sprinkle with 1/2 tsp salt. A spot in the stove to heat for 20 minutes until the butternut squash is delicate.

2. To prepare the kale, evacuate the stems and slash the leaves into chomp measured pieces. Spot the cleaved kale in an enormous plate of mixed greens bowl and sprinkle the leaves with a touch of salt. With clean hands rub the kale leaves by scrunching it between your hands for around 1 minute. The kale will wind up darker in shading chicken you do this.

3. Crush the cloves out of the broiled head of garlic and spot them in a blender or nutria bullet. Include the olive oil, balsamic, pepper, and discretionary egg yolk. Mix until smooth and rich.

4. To gather the plate of mixed greens place the destroyed kale in a bowl, top with the simmered butternut squash, broccoli, and red onion, top with the hacked almonds and toss with the dressing.

Nutrition Fact: Calories 166g, Fat 15g, Carbs 23g, Sugar 7g, Protein 4g

Whole30 Vegetarian Power Bowls

Prep Time: 10mins, Cooking Time: 40mins, Serving: 4

INGREDIENTS

For the Vegetables:

- 2 - tsp extra-virgin olive oil
- 1 - small red onion
- 2 - large sweet potatoes
- 2 - teaspoons chili powder
- ¾ - teaspoon salt
- ¾ - teaspoon black pepper
- 1 - small head broccoli
- 1 - small bunch kale

For the Dressing:

- 3 - tablespoons lemon juice
- 3 - tablespoons tahini
- 1 - clove garlic
- ½ -1 teaspoon ground cumin
- ¼ - teaspoon kosher salt
- 4 - hard-boiled eggs

INSTRUCTIONS

1. Spot a rack inside the focal point of your range and preheat the broiler to 400 tiers F. Generously coat a rimmed preparing sheet with a nonstick splash and put apart.

2. Spot the onions and sweet potatoes at the preparing sheet, turning the sweet potatoes cut aspects up. Shower with 2 teaspoons olive oil, ensuring the tissue of the sweet potatoes is all around blanketed. Sprinkle with 1 teaspoon bean stew powder, 1/four teaspoon salt, and 1/4 teaspoon pepper.

3. While the candy potatoes cook, hack the broccoli or cauliflower into florets. Expel the getting ready sheet from the stove and flip the sweet potatoes with the intention that they're chopped aspects down.

4. Expel the sheet skillet from the broiler and notice the kale over the vegetables. Shower the kale with the rest of the 2 teaspoons olive oil and sprinkle with residual 1/4 teaspoon salt and 1/four teaspoon pepper.

5. While vegetables get executed with cooking, installation the dressing: Add the lemon juice, tahini, garlic, cumin, and salt in a little mixing bowl. Include 2 tablespoons excessive temp water. Rush to sign up for.

Nutrition Fact: Calories 301.4g, Fat 17.6g, Carbs 6.9g, Sugars 3g, Protein 30.2g

Baked Eggs with Roasted Spring Vegetables

Prep Time: 10mins, Cooking Time: 30mins, Serving: 4-5

INGREDIENTS

- 1 - large Beet
- 2 - red Potatoes
- 1 - bunch radish
- Pinch of sea salt or kosher Salt
- Black Pepper to taste
- 2 - garlic cloves crushed
- 1–2 -tbsp Olive oil
- Lemon
- 1 zucchini
- 1 - Small Shallot
- 1–2 - cups leafy Greens
- England's Best eggs
- Fresh chopped herbs

INSTRUCTIONS

1. Preheat stove to 400 F.
2. Toss root vegetables in 1 tbsp oil, Pinch of ocean salt, dark pepper, and half of a lemon, squeezed. Cut the other portion of the lemon and spare lemon cuts for fixing.
3. Spot root vegetables on sheet container and dish in broiler at 400° for 15 to 20 minutes until delicate, however not overcooked.
4. Expel from the stove and spot the cut zucchini, slashed greens over the cooked vegetables. Season with salt pepper. You may likewise utilize spinach.
5. With a spatula, make 5 to 6 little hole in the skillet where you can put the eggs so the yolk doesn't break. Break the eggs over every fissure. In the event that you discover you have an egg with a running yolk, simply blend it to the container, yet chicken include another egg that has a set yolk. Or on the other hand, dispose of the running yolk. Layer cut lemon around th eggs
6. Sprinkle vegetables and eggs with discretionary ground parmesan. Spot skillet in the stove for 10-14 minutes or until egg whites has set. See notes. Heating times fluctuate with broiler and sort of skillet utilized.
7. Expel and trimming with herbs of the decision or slashed spring green onion.8. Serve immediately or scoop vegetable and eggs in water/air proof compartment and store in ice chest for some other time. Keeps well for 2 days in cooler.

Nutrition Fact: Calories 360g, Fat 24g, Carbs 34g, Sugars 1.4g, Protein 46g

Paleo Whole30 Cauliflower Fried Rice

Prep Time: 10mins, Cooking Time: 20mins, Servings 8-10

INGREDIENTS

- 1 - tablespoon ghee or coconut oil
- 1 - large red onion diced
- 4 - medium carrots shredded
- 10 - cloves garlic
- 3 - heads of cauliflower
- 1 ½ - teaspoons onion powder
- ¾ - teaspoon ground ginger
- 1 ¼ - teaspoons black pepper
- 1 ¼ - teaspoons sea salt
- 1/3 - cup coconut amino
- 1 - tablespoon apple cider vinegar
- 1 - teaspoon fish sauce omit for vegan
- 8 - eggs cooked & scrambled,
- green onions

INSTRUCTIONS

1. Warmth an enormous sauté dish on medium-high warmth for 2-3 minutes. Warmth up ghee includes diced onions and carrot. Cook until the onion looks translucent. Include garlic cloves and cook for an additional 30 seconds until fragrant.
2. Include riced cauliflower. Cautiously separate the cauliflower with a wooden spoon or spatula. Cook the rice until it looks delicate and delicate. This can take anyplace between 5-7 minutes.
3. Include the flavors until all around consolidated. Mix in coconut aminos, apple juice vinegar, and fish sauce. Cook on medium-high warmth until the cauliflower rice comes to your ideal doneness.
4. Cautiously mix in the scramble eggs. Mix for around 1 minute until everything has been very much consolidated. Expel from the warmth. Present with your preferred meat, fish or with eggs for breakfast.

Nutrition Fact: Calories 454g, Fat 6g, Carbs 9g, Sugars 1.2g, Protein 30.2g

Instant Pot Tahini Cashew Curry Recipe

Prep Time: 35mins, Cooking Time: 20mins, Serving: 2

INGREDIENTS

- 2 - cups Unsweetened Cashew Milk
- 3 - tablespoons Tahini Paste
- 2 - teaspoons Yellow Curry Paste

- 2 - teaspoons Fresh Ginger
- ½ - teaspoon Sea Salt
- 1 - tablespoon Turmeric
- 1 - tablespoon Tapioca Starch
- 1 - cup Cauliflower Florets
- ½ - cup Chopped Onion
- ½ - Red Bell Pepper
- Toasted Cashews
- Fresh Cilantro
- Rice of Choice

INSTRUCTIONS

1. Whisk each one of the fixings up to the custard starch collectively in your Instant Pot, set on sauté mode and warmth to the point of boiling.
2. Chicken effervescent, whisk the custard starch with 2 tablespoons of the new fluid together in a specific bowl until easy.
3. While usually whisking, blend the combination another time into the Instant pot until all around joined.
4. Heat up the curry till it starts to thicken and decrease, around 10mins, mixing as regularly as feasible.
5. Chicken thickened, blend in cauliflower, onion, and pepper. Spread the Instant Pot and prepare dinner on guide excessive weight for handiest 1 minute.
6. Give weight a risk to discharge usually.
7. On the off danger which you want the curry incredibly thicker, turn it returned to sauté and bubble 2-3mins.
8. Serve over rice of selection and enhancement with cashews and cilantro.

Nutrition Fact: Calories 430g, Fat 24g, Carbs 34g, Sugars 3g, Protein 26g

Caramelized Fennel, Leek & Onion Gratin

Prep Time: 20mins, Cooking Time: 25mins, Servings: 6

INGREDIENTS

- 2 - tbsp olive oil/coconut oil
- 3 - leeks thinly sliced
- 2 - white onions thinly sliced
- 2 - small fennel thinly sliced
- 2 - cloves garlic crushed
- ¼ - tsp salt
- ¾ - cup almond milk

- 1 - tbsp dijon mustard
- ½ - tsp pepper
- 2 - tbsp nutritional yeast
- 1 - cup vegetable/chicken stock
- 1 - tsp fresh thyme

INSTRUCTIONS

1. Preheat the broiler to a hundred seventy-five levels Celsius
2. In a brief blender encompass the depleted cashews and almond milk and blend till simply clean.
3. Empty the aggregate into a pot and embody the mustard, pepper, healthful yeast and stock.
4. It have to coat the lower back of a spoon.
5. Mix in 1 tsp crisp thyme
6. In a forged iron skillet warmness the oil on medium warmth and afterward consist of the leeks, onion, fennel and garlic.
7. Sprinkle with salt and depart to prepare dinner for 10 mins, till they become touchy, marginally caramelized and fantastic in shading.
8. Empty the cashew cream into the skillet and mix thru so it coats the majority of the veggies.
9. Move the skillet to the broiler and put together for 20 minutes till bubbly and notable on pinnacle.
10. Prior to serving sprinkle with crisp cleaved parsley or thyme.

Nutrition Fact: Calories 243g, Fat 6g, Carbs 4.6g, Sugars 1g, Protein 22g

Creamy Vegan Cauliflower Soup

Prep Time: 10mins, Cooking Time: 25mins, Serving: 4

INGREDIENTS

- 2 - tsp ghee coconut oil
- ½ - large yellow onion
- 4 - garlic cloves
- 1 - head of cauliflower washed
- 32 - ounces chicken
- 1 - sprig fresh rosemary
- 1 - tsp sea salt split in two
- ¾ - teaspoon dried chives
- 1 - teaspoon onion powder
- ½ - teaspoon smoked paprika

- 2 - ounces pancetta cubed
- sea salt to taste

INSTRUCTIONS

1. Spot a massive pot over medium-excessive warm temperature. Include the margarine, onion and garlic cloves and sauté for round 1 minute till aromatic.
2. Include cauliflower florets, stock, new rosemary and half of the salt.
3. Spread the pot, lower the warm temperature to medium and allow cook dinner for an additional 25mins, or until the cauliflower feels fork delicate.
4. While the cauliflower is cooking, add the pancetta to a bit sauté container over medium warm temperature.
5. Blending every once in a while, cook until the pancetta looks firm, around three-4 minutes. Move to a paper towel coated plate and put aside.
6. Chicken the cauliflower feels fork sensitive, evacuate the rosemary and include the the rest of the flavors and herbs and salt.
7. Move the soup combination into the Vitamin. Mix on medium-excessive until clean, around 30 seconds or via basically using the soup setting.
8. Empty the soup into serving bowls and embellishment with pancetta, coconut cream, and additional dried chives.

Nutrition Fact: Calories 331.5g, Fat 4.4g, Carbs 50.1g, Sugars 0.6g, Protein 25.7g

INSTANT POT SOUPS AND STEWS RECIPES

Instant Pot Taco Soup Recipe

Prep Time: 15mins, Cooking Time: 10mins, Serving: 6-8

INGREDIENTS

- 1 - pound ground beef
- 1 - bell pepper, diced
- 1 - medium onion, diced
- 3 - Tbsp paleo approved taco seasoning
- 1 - tsp garlic
- ¼ - tsp salt and pepper
- 14 - oz mild salsa
- 7 - oz diced green chilies
- lime juice from one fresh lime
- 4 - cups organic chicken broth

INSTRUCTIONS

1. Preheat Instant Pot on the Sauté setting.
2. Dark colored ground hamburger in the Instant Pot, breaking into little pieces with the back of your spoon.
3. Include diced Chile peppers, onions, and garlic, cooking just until starting to relax.
4. Include salsa, green bean stews, soup, lime squeeze, salt and pepper, and taco flavoring.
5. Turn Instant Pot off, and afterward back on. Utilizing the Manual or Soup setting, set clock to 10 minutes.
6. Make sure the valve is set to fix.
7. Permit a characteristic weight discharge for 10 minutes, at that point speedy discharge the rest of the weight.
8. Serve soup embellished with diced cilantro and cut an avocado.

Nutrition Fact: Calories 98g, Fat 5.1g, Carbs 11.7g, Sugars 1.3g, Protein 3.1g

Whole30 Creamy Taco Soup

Prep Time: 10mins, Cooking Time: 20mins, Serving: 6

INGREDIENTS

Soup:

- 1 ½ - tablespoons ghee
- 1 - large yellow onion

- 4 - bell peppers
- 2 - pounds grass fed beef
- 2-3 - tablespoons chili powder
- 2 - tablespoons cumin
- 2 - teaspoons sea salt
- 2 - teaspoons black pepper
- 1 - teaspoon paprika
- 1 - teaspoon cinnamon
- ½ - teaspoon garlic powder
- ½ - teaspoon onion powder
- 1/8 - ¼ tsp cayenne pepper
- 28 - ounces diced tomatoes
- 24 - ounces bone broth
- 5 - ounces coconut milk
- 8 - onces diced green chiles

INSTRUCTIONS

1. Liquefy the ghee to your Instant Pot.
2. Include the onions and chile peppers and sauté until delicate and sensitive.
3. This will take round five-7mins.
4. Include the grass-fed floor meat and mix until is cooked through and in no way again pink.
5. Channel the beef via a colander and re-upload it to the Instant Pot.
6. Include the general public of the flavors and mix properly.
7. Include diced tomatoes, stock, coconut milk, and inexperienced chiles and mix until very a lot consolidated.
8. Seal the Instant Pot cowl and select the "Soup" paintings.
9. Press the "- " capture to trade the cooking time to twenty-five minutes.
10. Chicken the soup is completed cooking, discharge the burden from your Instant Pot by way of converting the dial to the "Discharge" work.
11. Chicken the burden has all been discharged, open the top and consist of any or most of the people of the fixings recorded. Appreciate!

Nutrition Fact: Calories 75.6g, Fat 1.3g, Carbs 14.4g, Sugars 0.5g, Protein 5.1g

Lemon Garden Vegetable & Chicken Soup

Prep Time: 10mins, Cooking Time: 10mins, Serving: 4

INGREDIENTS

- 1 - tablespoon coconut oil
- 1 - pound chicken breasts
- 1 - leek yellow onion
- 3 - cloves garlic
- 2 - large carrots
- 2 - stalks of celery
- 1 - medium zucchini
- 1 - medium summer squash
- 1 - 14-ounce can diced tomatoes
- ½ - teaspoon dried rosemary
- ½ - teaspoon dried thyme
- Juice from 1 lemon
- 6 cups chicken broth
- ¼ - tsp salt & ground black pepper
- 2 - cups fresh baby spinach

INSTRUCTIONS

1. Warmth the coconut oil in the base of your Instant Pot on the sauté setting, and include the leeks/onion and garlic to the pot.

2. At the point chicken the leeks/onions are delicate, include the chicken, carrots, celery, zucchini, summer squash, canned tomatoes, rosemary, thyme, salt, pepper, and if utilizing, the asparagus and sugar snap peas. Pour in the soup and lemon squeeze, and mix.

3. Secure top on Instant Pot, and go to Soup setting. Set clock for 4 minutes, with the vent, fixed.

4. At the point chicken the clock goes off, discharge weight. Include spinach/kale and blend.

5. Serve in dishes and top each bowl with a solitary lemon cut. Serve hot! Goes extraordinary with a cut of without grain "Enticement" Bread.

Nutrition Fact: Calories 153.9g, Fat 0.6g, Carbs 33.5g, Sugars 2.7g, Protein 6.5g

Instant Pot AIP Paleo Chicken Fennel Soup

Prep Time: 20mins, Cooking Time: 30mins, Serving: 6-8

INGREDIENTS

- 1 - pound boneless, skinless chicken breast
- 1 - large bulb fennel
- ½ - onion
- 4 - green onions
- 1 - cup chopped kale or spinach
- 3 - cloves garlic
- 2 - cups chicken
- 4 - cups filtered water
- 1 - bay leaf
- 1 - tablespoon dried oregano
- 1/8 - teaspoon salt

INSTRUCTIONS

1. Add all fixings to Instant Pot.
2. Spot cover on the pot.
3. Press Soup catch.
4. Chicken cooking has halted, enable the pot to discharge weight normally for 10 minutes.
5. Open cover.
6. Serve.

Nutrition Fact: Calories 86.9g, Fat 3.5g, Carbs 11.2g, Sugars 1g, Protein 4.8g

Enchilada Chicken Stew

Prep Time: 10mins, Cooking Time: 8hrs, Serving: 4-6

INGREDIENTS

- 2 -lbs chicken breasts
- 1 - yellow onion
- 1 - green bell pepper
- 4 -oz of chopped jalapenos
- 4 -oz of chopped green chiles
- 2 - tablespoons coconut oil
- 14 -oz of diced tomatoes
- 7 - oz tomato sauce
- 3 - garlic cloves, minced

- 1 - tablespoon cumin
- 1 - tablespoon chili powder
- 2 - teaspoons dried oregano
- salt and pepper
- bundle of cilantro
- avocado, to garnish

INSTRUCTIONS

1. Take out your helpful dandy lazy cooker.
2. Incorporate your chook chests.
3. By chicken incorporate the rest of the fixings on top, in any solicitation.
4. Put on low for eight-10 hours or high for 6-eight.
5. After it's done the cooking, use tongs to choose on the chicken to shred it in with every last one of the fixings.
6. Top with cilantro and some avocado.
7. Eat up

Nutrition Fact: Calories 102.2g, Fat 6.3g, Carbs 11g, Sugars 2.2g, Protein 2.7g

Creamed Fennel and Cauliflower Soup

Prep Time: 20mins, Cooking Time: 10mins, Serving: 4

INGREDIENTS

For the salad:

- 1 - tablespoon coconut oil
- 1 - white onion
- 3 - cloves garlic
- 1 - extra-large fennel bulbs
- 1 - pound cauliflower florets
- 1 - cup coconut milk
- 3 - cups broth
- 2 - teaspoons salt
- Truffle oil, for serving
- Black pepper for serving

INSTRUCTIONS

1. Cut the onions, mince the garlic, and hack the fennel. In the event that your cauliflower isn't as of now cleaved into florets, do that now.
2. In the base of your weight cooker, heat up the coconut oil.

3. Sauté the onions until translucent. Include the garlic, fennel, and cauliflower. Sauté for 5-10 minutes, until the edges of the vegetables start to turn brilliant.

4. Pour the stock and coconut milk into the pot. Include salt. Cook on the soup setting for in any event 5 minutes.

5. Chicken the weight cooker is finished cooking, discharge the weight and evacuates the cover. Utilize a standing blender or an inundation blender to puree the soup to a smooth, velvety consistency.

6. Scoop into serving bowls and shower with truffle oil. Top with naturally wafer pepper, and topping with a left-over fennel frond. Serve hot.

Nutrition Fact: Calories 218g, Fat 12.9g, Carbs 7.6g, Sugars 1.4g, Protein 18.7g

PALEO EGG ROLL SOUP

Prep Time: 15mins, Cooking Time: 25mins, Serving: 4

INGREDIENTS:

- 1 - tablespoon ghee, avocado oil
- 1 - pound ground pastured pork
- 1 - large onion
- 32 -ounces chicken or beef broth
- ½ - head cabbage, chopped
- 2 - cups shredded carrots
- 1 - teaspoon garlic powder
- 1 - teaspoon onion powder
- 1 - teaspoon sea salt
- 1 - teaspoon ground ginger
- 2/3 - cup coconut amino

INSTRUCTIONS

1. In your Instant Pot dark colored the ground pork in the tablespoon of cooking fat with the diced onion; cook until never again pink

2. Include the rest of the fixings and cook for 25 minutes high weight chicken snappy discharge the weight

3. Evacuate top and serve

4. On the off chance that you need a thicker soup, evacuate 1/4 measure of juices from the soup and blend in 2-3 tablespoons of custard starch.

5. Reintroduce the slurry and mix well, it will thicken throughout the following couple of minutes

Nutrition Fact: Calories 76.6g, Fat 1.9g, Carbs 13.9g, Sugars 2.2g, Protein 1.8g

Pork and Napa Cabbage Soup

Prep Time: 10mins, Cooking Time: 10mins, Serving: 6

INGREDIENTS

- 1 - teaspoon ghee or fat of choice
- 1 - small onion
- Kosher salt
- 1 - pound ground pork
- 6 - large fresh shiitake mushrooms
- 2 - garlic cloves
- 6 - cups bone broth
- 1 - head Napa cabbage
- 2 - large carrots
- 1 - large russet potato
- Freshly ground black pepper
- 3 - scallions

INSTRUCTIONS

1. Warmth the ghee in a huge pot over medium warmth.
2. At the point chicken the fat is gleaming, toss in the diced onion with a sprinkle of salt.

Nutrition Fact: Calories 128.5g, Fat 2.5g, Carbs 21.2g, Sugars 3.5g, Protein 4.4g

Instant Pot Borscht Beet Soup

Prep Time: 20mins, Cooking Time: 40mins, Servings: 8

INGREDIENTS

- 1 - tbsp avocado oil
- 1.5 - lb beef stew meat
- 1 - large onion diced
- 4 - cups beef broth divided
- 2 - lb beets
- 2 - large carrots
- 1 - large russet potato
- 1 - small bunch dill
- Sea salt and black pepper

INSTRUCTIONS

1. Set the Instant Pot to Sauté. Include 1 tablespoon avocado oil.
2. Give the beef a risk to darker for around 5 minutes.

3. Include the diced onion and a pair of measures of the hamburger soup.

4. Spot the duvet at the Instant Pot, and set it to Manual for 30mins.

5. While the meat is cooking, prep the rest of the greens.

6. At the factor chicken the beef is completed, discharge the weight physically, evacuate the beef and onions with an opened spoon, and region it in a bowl to cool.

7. To the juices that are within the Instant Pot include: 2 extra mugs hamburger stock in addition to the beets, carrots, potato and dill.

8. Swap the top and prepare dinner for 6mins on Manual.

9. While this is cooking, shred the cooked meat with your hands.

10. At the factor chicken the veggies are completed cooking, discharge the load bodily.

11. Blend within the meat and adjust the seasonings with salt and pepper.

12. Serve adorned with a few cleaved dills.

Nutrition Fact: Calories 202.5g, Fat 5.7g, Carbs 13.9g, Sugars 1.4g, Protein 25.3g

Instant Pot Pork Chili Verde

Prep Time: 15mins, Cooking Time: 20mins, Serving: 5

INGREDIENTS

- 1 - Tbsp oil
- 1 - pound tomatillos
- 3 - cloves garlic
- ¾ - cup diced onion
- 2.5 - cups diced sweet potatoes
- 2 - Serrano peppers
- 2 - pounds pork stew meat
- ½ - cup broth
- 2–3 - Tbsp chopped cilantro

INSTRUCTIONS

1. Turn Instant Pot to sauté. Include all fixings aside from the soup and cilantro and sauté for 5 minutes, and after that mood killer.

2. Include stock and cilantro. Set Instant Pot for 20 minutes utilizing manual mode.

3. Utilize the brisk discharge strategy, blend well to support the sweet potatoes and tomatillos separate considerably further.

4. Serve warm! Discretionary garnishes incorporate avocado, salsa, cheddar, and so on.

Nutrition Fact: Calories 309.1g, Fat 12.3g, Carbs 7g, Sugars 0.8g, Protein 39.1g

CONCLUSION

I can't in any way, shape or form put sufficient accentuation in this basic truth the following 30 days will remodel you. It will change the way in that you consider sustenance. It will exchange your possibilities. It will change your propensities and your goals. It will reestablish a stable enthusiastic association with sustenance, and together with your body. It can likely alternate the way in that you eat for an incredible remainder. I recognize this because I did it, and a big number of individuals have performed it considering that, and it converted me and their lives in an emotional and changeless way.

www.ingramcontent.com/pod-product-compliance
Ingram Content Group UK Ltd.
Pitfield, Milton Keynes, MK11 3LW, UK
UKHW051133260726
13967UKWH00010B/3015

9 781801 219679